Reading Kazuo Ishiguro's *Never Let Me Go*

Reading Kazuo Ishiguro's Never Let Me Go*: The Alternative Dystopian Imagination* aims to offer innovative perspectives for the analysis of Nobel-prize winner Kazuo Ishiguro's oeuvre through a focus on the genre of science fiction, particularly the novel *Never Let Me Go* (2005). The study proposes the term "intimate dystopia" to reflect on the passage from totalitarian or external oppressive forces to more "subtle" systems of power. Its interdisciplinary approach combines, apart from literary theory on different genres such as science fiction and memory, race studies, feminism and ecocriticism. It is based on an exhaustive critical and textual analysis that allows for a thorough and nuanced understanding of Ishiguro's multi-layered novel, covering themes such as the ethical dimensions and gender implications of caregiving, the dystopian portrayal of the environment, the significance of art in the existence of marginalized groups and the genre-related complexities of the text.

Eva Pelayo Sañudo holds a PhD in gender and diversity from the University of Oviedo and currently teaches at the University of Cantabria (Spain). Her fields of research are American literature, ethnic, gender and postcolonial studies. Her monography *Spatialities in Italian American Women's Literature: Beyond the Mean Streets* (2021) has been awarded several prizes.

Routledge Focus on Literature

Margaret Wise Brown's Experimental Art
The Modernist Picture Book
Julia Pond

Tolkien and the Kalevala
Jyrki Korpua

Elevating Humanity via Africana Womanism
Clenora Hudson (Weems)

Reading Modernity, Modernism and Religion Today
Spinoza and Van Gogh
Patrick Grant

The Sagas of Icelanders
An Introduction to All Forty Sagas with Summaries
Annette Lassen

Pandemics and Apocalypse in World Literature
The Hope for Planetary Salvation
William Franke

Reading Kazuo Ishiguro's *Never Let Me Go*
The Alternative Dystopian Imagination
Eva Pelayo Sañudo

For more information about this series, please visit: www.routledge.com/Routledge-Focus-on-Literature/book-series/RFLT

Reading Kazuo Ishiguro's *Never Let Me Go*

The Alternative Dystopian Imagination

Eva Pelayo Sañudo

NEW YORK AND LONDON

First published 2025
by Routledge
605 Third Avenue, New York, NY 10158

and by Routledge
4 Park Square, Milton Park, Abingdon, Oxon, OX14 4RN

Routledge is an imprint of the Taylor & Francis Group, an informa business

Library of Congress Cataloging-in-Publication Data
Names: Pelayo Sañudo, Eva, author.
Title: Reading Kazuo Ishiguro's Never let me go : the alternative dystopian imagination / Eva Pelayo Sañudo.
Description: New York, NY : Routledge, 2025. | Series: Routledge focus on literature | Includes bibliographical references and index.
Identifiers: LCCN 2024043281 (print) | LCCN 2024043282 (ebook) | ISBN 9781032870533 (hardback) | ISBN 9781032870540 (paperback) | ISBN 9781003530695 (ebook)
Subjects: LCSH: Ishiguro, Kazuo, 1954- Never let me go. | LCGFT: Literary criticism.
Classification: LCC PR6059.S5 N4838 2025 (print) | LCC PR6059.S5 (ebook) | DDC 823/.914--dc23/eng/20240926
LC record available at https://lccn.loc.gov/2024043281
LC ebook record available at https://lccn.loc.gov/20240432

ISBN: 9781032870533 (hbk)
ISBN: 9781032870540 (pbk)
ISBN: 9781003530695 (ebk)

DOI: 10.4324/9781003530695

Typeset in Times New Roman
by KnowledgeWorks Global Ltd.

Contents

Introduction to Kazuo Ishiguro's Writing and His "Intimate Dystopia" *Never Let Me Go*

Contemporary writers continue to engage in the tradition of the dystopian imagination. For example, in *Dystopian Literature: A Theory and Research Guide* (Cooker 1994), numerous dystopias are surveyed and even recent examples by Margaret Atwood and Haruki Murakami are included. However, in view of the existence of more works fitting the genre, research needs to be updated. Particularly, considering Kazuo Ishiguro would be a critical gain due to his acclaimed text *Never Let Me Go* (2006/2005) and even *Klara and the Sun* (2021), his more recent science-fiction novel since winning the Nobel Prize in Literature in 2017.

As a matter of fact, *Never Let Me Go* (further references in the text abbreviated as *NLMG*) was not only short-listed for the prestigious Booker Prize but won the Arthur C. Clarke Award, in addition to the National Book Critics Circle Award as one of "the finest books published in English".[1] It is this remarkable contribution to dystopian fiction to which this book-length study responds. Furthermore, Ishiguro is one of the most acclaimed writers "of our time" due to his best-selling works which attract global praise in terms of criticism and readership (Groes and Lewis 2011, 1). Following also his contemporary Haruki Murakami, "It is a joy to be blessed with a contemporary like [him]" (2010, 8).

There have been some attempts at assessing the growing impact of Kazuo Ishiguro's oeuvre in contemporary writing such as through the international conference "Kazuo Ishiguro and the International Novel", held at Liverpool Hope University in 2007, or the books *Kazuo Ishiguro in a Global Context* (Wong and Hülya 2016) and *Kazuo Ishiguro: New Critical Visions of the Novels* (Groes and Lewis 2011). Yet there are no extended studies on the author which focus on the genre of science fiction.

This book deals with innovative methods of reading or analyzing the dystopic world presented in Kazuo Ishiguro's novel *NLMG*, such as by providing an intersectional perspective of the identity categories of class, gender and race, which is addressed in the first chapter. Next, the study concentrates on new forms of representing dystopic settings by decentering the role of the urban space in environmental criticism. Furthermore, chapter three analyzes original themes such as how the persistence of hope may be present even in dystopias, while the

DOI: 10.4324/9781003530695-1

final chapter examines unique writing techniques by handling blended narrative forms that combine the verisimilitude of autobiography with the speculation of the genre of science fiction.

The study is based on an interdisciplinary perspective combining race studies, postcolonial theory, feminism and ecocriticism, as well as literary theory on different genres such as science fiction and memory. This offers an all-encompassing scope that is adequately organized in separate chapters, making it attractive for different areas of research and fit to address specific educational purposes. It balances a broad, overview approach with the ability, in each chapter, to offer topical insights that are either completely new or offer argumentative summaries of how scholarship has dealt with a particular topic in relation to the novel.

The novel in question deserves special attention as it is particularly distinctive in the context of the author's oeuvre as a science fiction text while still perfectly fitting in many of the social themes displayed in his other novels. In fact, the study also enlarges criticism about Japan-born British and Nobel-prize winner Kazuo Ishiguro, who is yet considered among the "rare instances of Anglophone writers of the Asian diaspora using the themes and conventions of science fiction" (Goh 2010, 45). In other words, although the genre has been a canonical form of European and American writing, few diasporic or racialized authors have achieved international renown within the Western "markets that dominate the production and consumption of science fiction" (46). This makes Ishiguro a unique writer and particularly situates *NLMG* as a fundamental text of great interest for science fiction readers and scholars.

As explained above, the author's reception within the world of science fiction has considered his racial background as a British writer of Japanese descent. In addition, the novel has been read through the prism of race. For example, one review stated that the novel "is a masterpiece of racial metaphor" in that its "characters may not be Asian, but the book is an incisive commentary on nonwhite experience" (Wong 2018, n.p.). Ishiguro was born in Nagasaki, Japan, but when he was six, he moved to Surrey, England. He became well-known for his third novel, *The Remains of the Day*, published in 1989, which also won the Booker Prize and was adapted into a film starring Anthony Hopkins and Emma Thompson. In the same year, 1989, he revisited for the first time Japan, according to the "Chronology of Kazuo Ishiguro's life" where no further references to his Asian heritage are mentioned (Matthews and Groes 2011, xi–xv). Furthermore, Japanese identity appears to figure scarcely or at least not overtly in his writing, which has been labeled as composed of "'English' fictions par excellence" and mostly apolitical (Neagu 2010, 269).

Nonetheless, the reception of *NLMG* in racial terms has not only been noticed in the review just shown, given that critics have also addressed the novel's reflection of contemporary social problems usually faced by minorities, among others, as it will be further discussed in the next chapter. In addition, the text can offer an innovative perspective that differs from most dystopias (and even utopias or science fiction in general) in which criticism of society shows little concern with the intricacies of gender either (Monk 1980) until women writers started to redress the androcentric portrayal of the genre ever since the late 1970s and 1980s (Armitt 2012, 1). For this reason, I will look closely at what I term Ishiguro's "intimate dystopia" which means that, unlike most fictions, totalitarian or external oppressive forces are decentered in favor of more "subtle" systems of power. In other words, it is a dystopia where the intimate and commonly femininized acts of caring and reproduction are instrumentalized to harvest human clones.

Note

1 The National Book Critics Circle Awards: https://www.bookcritics.org/awards/.

References

Armitt, Lucie. 2012. *Where No Man Has Gone Before: Essays on Women and Science Fiction*. New York: Routledge.

Cooker, Keith. 1994. *Dystopian Literature: A Theory and Research Guide*. Westport: Greenwood Press.

Goh, Robbie. 2010. "The Postclone-nial in Kazuo Ishiguro's *Never Let Me Go* and Amitav Ghosh's *The Calcutta Chromosome*: Science and the Body in the Asian Diaspora." *Ariel: A Review of International English Literature* 41.3–4: 45–71.

Groes, Sebastian, and Barry Lewis. 2011. *Kazuo Ishiguro: New Critical Visions of the Novels*. London: Red Globe Press.

Ishiguro, Kazuo. 2006/2005. *Never Let Me Go*. Kent: Faber and Faber.

Ishiguro, Kazuo. 2021. *Klara and the Sun*. New York: Knopf.

Matthews, Sean, and Sebastian Groes, eds. 2010. *New Critical Visions of the Novels*. London: Red Globe Press.

Monk, Patricia. 1980. "Frankenstein's Daughters: The Problems of the Feminine Image in Science Fiction." *Mosaic: A Journal for the Interdisciplinary Study of Literature* 13.3–4: 15–27.

Murakami, Haruki. 2010. "Foreword: On Having a Contemporary Like Kazuo Ishiguro". In *New Critical Visions of the Novels*, edited by Sean Matthews and Sebastian Groes, vii–xix. London: Red Globe Press.

Neagu, Adriana. 2010. "International Writing? Kazuo Ishiguro and the Introvert Identities of the Novel." *English* 59.226: 269–280.

Wong, Mimi. 2018. "Kazuo Ishiguro's '*Never Let Me Go*' Is a Masterpiece of Racial Metaphor". Available at: https://electricliterature.com/kazuo-ishiguros-never-let-me-go-is-a-masterpiece-of-racial-metaphor/

Wong, Cynthia, and Yildiz Hülya, eds. 2016. *Kazuo Ishiguro in a Global Context*. New York: Routledge.

1 Gendered Capitalism

A Critical Analysis of Educational, Economic and Cultural Systems

Ishiguro's dystopic world in *Never Let Me Go* (*NLMG*; 2006/2005) establishes important critical engagements which allow us to explore contemporary problems in our societies. Apart from delving into the existential questions and conflicts typical to the genre, the novel portrays familiar inequalities in terms of gender, class and race, which reflect disheartening issues humanity must acknowledge and confront. This approach allows us to critically interpret our world and possibly envision the capacity for change. Following De Villiers and Slabbert, it

> confronts us with a world that is foreign to us and with that which is *other* to ourselves. This confrontation with otherness affords us the opportunity to expose ill-conceived schematizations and to generate new insight in order to understand ourselves and the status quo better.
>
> (2011, 87; emphasis original)

This chapter focuses on the value of bodies within capitalist, racist and gendered systems. First, the manufacture of "perfect" bodies in the economy of cloning is shown through the emphasis on sports, health and chastity. From an early age, the characters are exposed to an intense educational program and other cultural beliefs that work to their exploitation. In other words, they endure a type of "brainwashing" typical of dystopias (Cappo 2009, 48). Second, the inequalities of this perverse system are also portrayed in how characters are further segregated and dehumanized and how their treatment has been compared to the situation of immigrants, minorities and poor people (Gill 2014). Finally, the production of gender differences is also obvious through the representation of sexuality, femininity and heterosexuality. Nonetheless, the novel also presents the imaginative potential of caring, typically a devalued woman's role, for creating new and challenging dystopian mythologies. In doing so, Ishiguro's text offers a critical reading that can shape our capacity to solve the vexing problems of humanity.

DOI: 10.4324/9781003530695-2

The Value of Bodies: Sports, Health and Chastity

In general terms, *NLMG* is a story about genetic engineering set in an alternative England in the late 1990s. Kathy H. is the narrator who is in her 30s but approaching the end of her life, and so remembers her childhood and especially her relationship with her two best friends Tommy and Ruth. Kathy describes herself as a "carer", which is the previous role before she becomes "a donor", such as her own friends whom she takes care of. All the characters are undergoing "donations" of their organs until they "complete", the euphemism for dying given that, as it becomes obvious, they are human clones who are "bred to produce healthy organs, organs that belonged to society" (Hyvärinen 2008, 217). Apart from suffering blatant exploitation at the service of reproductive technologies, the act of caring is clearly instrumentalized:

> Before having their organs *harvested*, the clones spend a period as carers, during which they drive around the country attending to the needs of donors and acting as their advocates. The narrator is Kathy H., herself a clone, acting as a carer at the time of the narrative.
>
> (Stacy 2015, 238; emphasis mine)

In this respect, *NLMG* has been compared to similar novels about the potential nightmares of eugenics programs (e.g. Aldous Huxley's *Brave New World*, 1932) and to feminist dystopias such as Margaret Atwood's *The Handmaid's Tale* (1985), which depicts "the plight of a woman in a world where biological reproduction has been hijacked by a totalitarian state" (McDonald 2007, 76). Accordingly, the novel shows the crucial value of the characters' bodies within the profitable market of cloning (only the richer can afford the service) and their gradual awareness that they are therefore "different":

> "You've been told about it. You're students. You're... special. So keeping yourselves well, keeping yourselves very healthy inside, that's much more important for each of you than it is for me [...]" We certainly knew—though not in any deep sense—that we were different from our guardians, and also from the normal people outside; we perhaps even knew that a long way down the line there were donations waiting for us.
>
> (Ishiguro 2006/2005, 68–9)

The passage presents a hierarchical society divided into students, guardians and normal people. The guardians are the students' tutors or teachers in the boarding school of Hailsham,[1] where rules are mostly established to ensure the pupils' proper work as clones. This explains why not only "at Hailsham the guardians were really strict about smoking" but also the intense indoctrination through formal education:

> There was even a rumor that some classic books—like the Sherlock Holmes ones—weren't in our library because the main characters smoked too much, and when you came across a page torn out of an illustrated book or magazine, this was because there'd been a picture on it of someone smoking. And then there were the actual lessons where they showed us horrible pictures of what smoking did to the insides of your body.
>
> (67)

Students also attend lessons about sex with a "life-size skeleton from the biology class" (82), through which they learn to dissociate sexuality from reproduction as well as their essential difference from humans. Most importantly, even though clones are unable to reproduce, chastity is stressed for the sake of being kept healthy: "they were telling us how we'd have to be very careful to avoid diseases when we had sex, it would have been odd not to mention how much more important this was for us than for normal people outside" (82). Students not only receive contradictory messages that confuse them about the nature of sex (also described as a natural or even beautiful need) but their sexual freedom is carefully managed through institutional control:

> the guardians made it more or less impossible for any of us actually to do much without breaking rules. We couldn't visit the boys' dorms after nine o'clock, they couldn't visit ours. The classrooms were all officially "out of bounds" in the evenings, as were the areas behind the sheds and the pavilion [...] In other words, for all the talk of sex being beautiful, we had the distinct impression we'd be in trouble if the guardians caught us at it.
>
> (93)

At the same time, given the insistence on contrasting Hailsham and the outside world, chastity is also a convenient means to avoid miscegenation and any kind of contact or attachment clone-human:

> Then suddenly, with the skeleton in an obscene heap on the desktop, she turned away and began telling us how we had to be careful who we had sex with. Not just because of the diseases, but because, she said, "sex affects emotions in ways you'd never expect". We had to be extremely careful about having sex in the outside world, especially with people who weren't students, because out there sex meant all sorts of things.
>
> (82)

As a result of being kept in this ignorance, students come up with different "theories" to try to explain who they are and the social relations of the world they live in (46–7). When finding about their being clones, "the possibles theory" expresses their desire to find the "normals" after which they "were modelled from" (137). Moreover, sex is differently interpreted as an obstacle to their role as donors, as a mark of their difference ("normal" sex implies to have babies) and as a way to cross borders both at Hailsham (between students and teachers) and outside. This reflects the power exerted over students to control their bodies from an early age, particularly through the educational system, which is not a path to knowledge, self-fulfillment and equality but a form to maintain a certain status quo.

Students are brought up to accept their destinies and identity as nonhuman donors. According to the veteran guardians, who see themselves as reformists by having initiated a "very vocal movement" (256), students' seclusion is also justified as a way to protect them from society's evils and to particularly demonstrate peculiar perceptions of their humanity. This is sought and promoted through the Gallery, an exhibition of students' work for the development of artistic skills that can "reveal" their souls:

> why would anyone doubt you had a soul? But I have to tell you, my dear, it wasn't something commonly held when we first set out all those years ago. And though we've come a long way since then, it's still not a notion universally held, even today. [...] All around the country, at this very moment, there are students being reared in deplorable conditions, conditions you Hailsham students could hardly imagine. [...] we at least saw to it that all of you in our care, you grew up in wonderful surroundings. [...] Most importantly we demonstrated to the world that if students were reared in humane, cultivated environments, it was possible for them to grow to be as sensitive and intelligent as any ordinary human being. Before that, all clones—or *students*, as we preferred to call you—existed only to supply medical science [...] that's largely all you were to most people. Shadowy objects in test tubes.
>
> (255–6)

However, in "The Failure of Humanizing Education in Kazuo Ishiguro's *Never Let Me Go*", society's mistreatment toward the nonhuman is completely rejected, including the institutions' presumed intentions, namely that "Hailsham's political mission is the humanization of the students through securing recognition of their humanity from the outside world" (Snaza 2015, 215). Certainly, that recurrent (re)production of social difference and the representation of hierarchical positions of power strongly disclaim such "a civilizing mission". As it is well argued: "Despite the fact that the students seem to exhibit human traits, they are nevertheless killed for their organs [...]

The students in the novel are never recognized as human, they are only spare parts *for* humans" (215; emphasis original). The fact that students are reduced to their material role as donors can be interpreted from postcolonial theory and the concepts of dehumanization and othering, which function as a recurrent practice to justify their exploitation by the social elite or dominant groups (Aschroft et al. 1998; Hawley and Nelson 2001). This framework illuminates the reduction of the characters to their bodies and the degradation of their subjectivity and humanity, which also elucidates their ultimate status as slaves, just the same as postcolonial subjects (Ikas 2017), as critics have argued.

According to Rachel Carroll, even though the subculture of a boarding school represents a recognizable narrative of childhood and identity formation for the reader, she stresses that "the rituals of child and adolescent cultures are implicated in this novel in what is essentially an institution of biotechnological slavery" (2010, 7). Other authors have also compared slavery and genetic engineering due to the "commodification of the body" (Everett 2003, 58), which explains why the characters in Ishiguro's novel are so controlled and disciplined. Furthermore, we might pinpoint other examples of the segregation and dehumanization to which students are subject, how they are "kept in the shadows" and perceived as "less than human" (Ishiguro 2006/2005, 258). Following a postcolonial analysis once more, "the clones are excluded and discriminated to be 'the other' from the normal people. The manifestations of othering in *Never Let Me Go* can be presented in the forms of linguistic features, indoctrination, objectification, and assimilation" (Vichiensing 2017, 126). There are more examples of exclusion and dehumanization which compare the clones' situation to the treatment of the underprivileged in our society.

Spatial Segregation and Dehumanization

According to Rosemarie Garland-Thomson, it is "urgent" to address global concerns such as the issue of organ trafficking portrayed in *NLMG*, which reflects "the inequality of bodies" of our contemporary world (2019, 31). As Franziska Quabeck also notes, the novel needs to be critically analyzed beyond the obvious ethical implications of cloning. She contends that attention may be focused on the exploration of contemporary problems in our societies, particularly regarding the deprived status and lack of rights of many minorities:

> Kazuo Ishiguro's *Never Let Me Go* seems to be, *prima facie*, about the ethical ramifications of human cloning, but a closer look at the narrative suggests a reading that reveals the difficulties of identity formation in people who are segregated and oppressed.
>
> (2017, 214)

Described as "an allegory on the lives of minorities in the present day" (214), we are now to concentrate on the novel's representation of spatial and discursive practices that contribute to the segregation and dehumanization of the "other" in *NLMG* and in our societies. As Bruce Robbins additionally points out, "the organ donation gulag, tucked away from public view and yet not kept fully secret, has its obvious real-world counterpart in what we call class" (2007, 200).

David Sibley has studied this problem in his research about the "geographies of exclusion" (2002). He has identified the practice of "Mapping the Pure and the Defile" in which he argues that the fear and exclusion of social difference have been spatially sanctioned and reinforced:

> There is a history of imaginary geographies which cast minorities, "imperfect" people, and a list of others who are seen to pose a threat to the dominant group in society as polluting bodies or folk devils who are then located "elsewhere". This "elsewhere" might be nowhere, as when genocide or the moral transformation of a minority like prostitutes are advocated, or it might be some spatial periphery, like the edge of the world or the edge of the city.
>
> (2002, 49)

In other words, traditional forms of ghetto living are not a spontaneous phenomenon or deliberate choice but a powerful instrument to fend off individuals who are just perceived as different or deviant from the norm. This social division through space also resonates in *NLMG*. Another important institutional rule at Hailsham which tries to ensure the neat division with the world outside is that of never trespassing beyond the Woods. Perhaps this choice is all the more convenient as the setting of the Woods has been used as a symbol of everything-one-must-fear in stories for children from the beginning of time. This spatial segregation is maintained not only through specific or strict norms but through education or the (re)production of cultural beliefs, as with the issue of health. In this case, the feeling of fear functions as an apt deterrent Valentine (1989)[2]: "There were all kinds of horrible stories about the woods" (Ishiguro 2006/2005, 25). Following Ivan Stacy, the remarkable "circulation of unreliable beliefs" with a similar outlook serves a clear purpose:

> These stories help to secure the clones' place in the organ donation program by acting as a form of self-regulation. One rumor tells of a boy who left the site, and whose body was later found tied to a tree with its hands and feet cut off; another describes how a girl, having left, was forbidden to return by the guardians […] and how her ghost has since haunted the woods.
>
> (2015, 222)

Students are also severely restricted in their mobility as they lack any basic knowledge about geography or where they live in the country, which unsurprisingly is not transmitted through education either: "For all our map lessons with Miss Emily, we had no real idea at that point about distances and how easy or hard it was to visit a particular place" (Ishiguro 2006/2005, 116).

As seen before, students repeatedly seem to question the norms by coming up with theories about what they are told. Their ongoing search for answers disclaims the idea that they are purely "automatic and mechanized" beings "without the capacity to resist their own exploitation" (Black 2009, 788). However, they are too young to completely understand their lives and have few sources of information and agents of socialization:

> Thinking back now, I can see we were just at that age when we knew a few things about ourselves—about who we were, how we were different from our guardians, from the people outside—but hadn't yet understood what any of it meant.
>
> (Ishiguro 2006/2005, 36)

In addition, they have mostly internalized their position in Hailsham or society as a result of the subtle forms in which power works, as Michel Foucault (2000/1975, 2007/1976) theorized through the concepts of the panopticon and biopower to explain individual self-control and surveillance. In the novel, both norms and cultural beliefs regulate students' behavior:

> But did we really believe in the Gallery? Today, I'm not sure. As I've said, we never mentioned it to the guardians and looking back, it seems to me this was a rule we imposed on ourselves, as much as anything the guardians had decided. I'm sure somewhere in your childhood, you too had an experience like ours that day; similar if not in the actual details, then inside, in the feelings.
>
> (Ishiguro 2006/2005, 32)

As a consequence, it is only in retrospect and once they leave Hailsham that students can finally grasp some elemental critical understanding of themselves and social relations. Through Kathy's recurring practice of "thinking back", the feelings of alienations are more accurately understood as a reflection of their being treated as outsiders. For example, dehumanization is abruptly shown through animalization:

> Madame *was* afraid of us. But she was afraid of us in the same way someone might be afraid of spiders. We hadn't been ready for that. It had never occurred to us to wonder how *we* would feel, being seen like that, being the spiders.
>
> (35; emphasis original)

Madame further objectifies them with her repeated paternalism such as when calling them "poor creatures", as "creature" denotes disgust and strangeness, which certainly stigmatizes the other, emphasizing "that clones are merely the underclass" (Guo 2015, 5). According to Rebecca Walkovitz's critique of anthropocentrism and objectification, a deliberate hierarchy is established to make acceptable or sustain the sacrifice of nonhuman beings: "the donation system functions because the humans see the clones as non individuated organisms, like radios or spiders" (2007, 225).

These discursive practices, which have been often used to legitimize dominance over marginalized people like immigrants or colonized people, are not innocuous but have a great power on the individual's subjectivity and alienation. Kathy understands her otherness through a "double-vision" (Goh 2011, 63), that is, that external perception or recognition which, following postcolonial theory (Hall 1987; McLeod 2000), generates cultural narratives about us that escape our control:

> the moment when you realize that you really are different to them; that there are people out there, like Madame, who don't hate you or wish you any harm, but who nevertheless shudder at the very thought of you—of how you were brought into this world and why—and who dread the idea of your hand brushing against theirs. The first time you glimpse yourself through the eyes of a person like that, it's a cold moment. It's like walking past a mirror you've walked past every day of your life, and suddenly it shows you something else, something troubling and strange.
>
> (Ishiguro 2006/2005, 36)

This distorted and external perception is better explained through the Du Boissian concept of "double-consciousness", which has also been paramount in race studies to theorize the formation of their subordinated identity. In *The Souls of Black Folk*, he exposes a description which is very similar to Kathy's experience: "It is a peculiar sensation, this double-consciousness, this sense of always looking at one's self through the eyes of others, of measuring one's soul by the tape of a world that looks on in amused contempt and pity" (2007/1903, 8). For this reason, the classic motif of the mirror, a symbol of identity, reveals the split and deep distortion of subjectivity as an important consequence of that discursive dominance, which has the "power to make us see and experience ourselves as 'Other'" (Hall 1998, 226). Prejudice against the students/clones is actually general at Hailsham and is shown by the same feelings of "revulsion" and "dread" toward them: "We're *all* afraid of you" (Ishiguro 2006/2005, 264; emphasis original).

In the outer world, they are also perceived to be strange or suspect when not blatantly ignored. Humans do not seem to pay much attention to the students/clones on the few occasions in which their paths cross, which proves how there is an "unbridgeable gap between the clones and the world of adult vocation, in full sight of one another and yet isolated" (Rosenfeld 2005, 137–8). As a matter of fact, their alienation increases when they feel that, being clones or copies of other humans, they are based on the most marginal members of society, as Ruth denounces: "We're modelled from *trash*. Junkies, prostitutes, winos, tramps. Convicts, maybe, just so long as they aren't psychos. That's what we come from" (Ishiguro 2006/2005, 164; emphasis original). As there is no evidence in the novel to confirm this belief, it actually proves "the distorted image they have of themselves: [...] the deeply internalized demeaning picture of themselves that society has imprinted on their souls" (Quabeck 2017, 221).

To face discrimination, the characters often resort to strategies of assimilation, particularly in their occasional "visits" to the outside world as they try to "pass" as "normals". In fact, they are much expected to lose their identity and accommodate to mainstream models given their further instruction in "Culture Briefing", that is, "classes where we had to role play various people we'd find out there—waiters in cafés, policemen and so on" (Ishiguro 2006/2005, 108). However, the efforts to assimilate into mainstream society are also linked to the feminist concept of performativity, showing the constructed nature of identity and opening new possibilities for constructing alternative utopias.

The Ethics of Caring as a (Feminist) Utopia

Although set in a dystopic context, Ishiguro's novel reflects the familiar (re)production of gender differences we find in our societies. This is especially shown in the efforts to display traditional forms of sexuality, femininity and heterosexuality, which according to the feminist concept of performativity serves to normalize gender identity and relations (Butler 2022/2021).

The novel addresses themes and dilemmas that tend to appear in the literature depicting common processes of becoming adults or maturing. First, Kathy confesses typical contradictions of sexuality in youth, such as the urgency to be sexually active and repression. On the one hand, she is concerned about what can be understood as the group's pressure, which advocates sexual freedom, given that "two of the girls I was closest to definitely had done it. Laura with Rob D., even though they'd never been a proper couple. And Ruth with Tommy" (Ishiguro 2006/2005, 96). In general, therefore, although being in a couple could be desirable, sex is felt as something "you ought to [do], and quickly" (96). On the other hand, she is also repressed by adults' conception of sex, that is, more in accordance with social norms: "For all that, I'd been holding it off for ages, repeating to myself Miss Emily's advice—'If you can't find someone with whom you truly wish to share this experience, then *don't!*'" (96; emphasis original). At the same time, other traditional views about sexuality circulates among students themselves such as when Ruth critiques Kathy's sexual freedom to distance her from Tommy on the grounds that he "doesn't like girls who've been with...

well, you know, with this person and that" (197). Lastly, Kathy herself seems to hold negative views about her sexuality, as she links it to pornography magazines when looking for her possible, thinking that her model, and therefore the explanation for her sexual desire, could be there.

Second, heterosexual relations are seen as the norm as opposed to the "confusion" of homosexuality, dismissed as "umbrella sex" or "gay stuff" (94). Furthermore, Kathy detects the imitation of dominant love relationships in some "veteran couples at the Cottages",[3] whose "mannerisms were copied from the television" (118). In turn, those couples are imitated by Tommy and Ruth, who act like "they were in a play" and become "more or less exactly like the veteran couples" (119). The formers' displays of affection are felt as somehow artificial or "showy in public" (118).

Performativity and heteronormativity are also reinforced by the belief that couples get "deferrals", that is, their donations could be postponed if they "prove" that they're "properly" in love (150). Following Rachel Carroll, the need for such a proof means that "desires and attachments between students are credible only so far as they emulate those of 'normals'" (2010, 19). However, Carroll has also identified the queerness of the novel in representing "non-normative heterosexuality", which she defines as a "heterosexual identity which is disempowered and marginalized by heteronormativity" (3). She thus explains the students' fundamental difference as clones in their inability to reproduce, which determines dominant constructions of heterosexuality given that conception has been naturalized, whereas sterility or infertility is conceived as artificial or a pathology (Steinberg 1997):

> in the disciplinary context of the classroom, the students are instructed in the inferiority of their identities. They are informed unambiguously that sex is more meaningful where it can result in conception and birth, something that none of them will experience; hence, their sexuality and desires are constructed as poor imitations of those of the "normals".
>
> (15)

The importance of reproduction is emphasized by the song which gives title to the novel: "Oh baby, baby, never let me go". Kathy misunderstands the song lyrics (where "baby" would refer to a "lover") and interprets it as the story about "a woman who'd been told she couldn't have babies, who'd really, really wanted them all her life. Then there's a sort of miracle and she has a baby" (Ishiguro 2006/2005, 70). Such misunderstanding could well imply a sort of identification with her own desires, given that while rejoicing in "play[ing] my song again and again" (70), she also replicates the typical acts of motherhood or pregnancy: "what I was doing was swaying about slowly in time to the song, holding an imaginary baby to my breast. In fact, [...] I'd grabbed a pillow to stand in for the baby" (71).

This central "imitation of life" in the novel signs the close connection of the characters with humanity and so points toward "the discursive reproduction of the human as a contested category of identity" (Carroll 2010, 3). In other words, Kathy is (re)producing unequivocable acts that are perceived as human, which is the reason she evokes ambivalent feelings of empathy and fear in the guardian who casually "attends her performance". She is surprised by Madame who "went on standing out there, sobbing and sobbing, staring at me through the doorway with that same look in her eyes she always had when she looked at us, like she was seeing something that gave her the creeps" (Ishiguro 2006/2005, 35).

Hence, more than art, reproduction seems to determine what it means to be human and points to the disempowered and dispossessed position of Kathy and her friends in such a dystopic world where they are merely instrumentalized bodies. In turn, Kathy continues to adhere to the significance of the role when she believes that "Madame is sorry for her because her maternal instinct will be thwarted: the clones have been doomed to childlessness" (Toker and Chertoff 2008, 168). However, the novel also reimagines traditional female roles, particularly caring, for challenging dystopian mythologies or, perhaps, as a (feminist) utopia.

Caring is the very first concept found in *NLMG*, an over-repeated word in which professionalism is gradually replaced by the language of affect: "The novel asks whether, within a radically materialist society that reduces humans to collections of organs or body parts, a language of care can still be articulated, and if so, where such a language might be located" (Whitehead 2011, 63).

The alternative to the dystopian dehumanization explained above could well be expressed through Kathy as she defines the *work* of caring as a profoundly emotional and personal bond, that is, away from the capitalist blindness to codependence and the elemental task of care that sustains us all. Traditionally, the act of caring, which is generally gendered as it is considered a woman's role, has not been economically compensated nor considered as work properly.

> Unpaid care work is both an important aspect of economic activity and an indispensable factor contributing to the well-being of individuals, their families and societies [...] Despite this importance for well-being, unpaid care work is commonly left out of policy agendas due to a common misperception that, unlike standard market work measures, it is too difficult to measure and less relevant for policies.
>
> (Ferrant et al. 2014, 1)

One of the reasons caring has been traditionally ignored and undervalued is precisely because of the underlying gendered conceptualization, as said before.

There is not only a gender gap in that care work is mostly assumed by women, but there is also an epistemological legitimation:

> "care work" is usually devalued as a social activity or practice, and is also devalued conceptually through its assumed connection with privacy, with emotion and with the "needy". Because our society treats public accomplishment, rationality, and autonomy as worthy qualities, care is devalued as it embodies their opposites.
>
> (19)

However, this has been challenged by a recent paradigm shift in feminism which revalues traditionally disregarded women's tasks and particularly places nurturing and caring at the center in contexts largely ruled by economic and labor demands (Himmelweit and Plomien 2014; Sevenhuijsen 2003). Western societies have experienced a transition from the private dimension of caring, which used to be a task most women did in exchange for nothing or "out of love", to "the rise of professional care service industries" (Folbre and Nelson 2000, 127). This means that caring is, apart from paid, more valued as it demands "more skilled and emotionally complex dimensions" (126). This comprehensive shift in the conceptualization of caring is present in *NLMG:*

> Kathy's opening remarks locate the word within discourses of professionalism and competency. Looking back over her eleven years as a carer, she considers that she has been good at her job, both in her own judgment and in the eyes of her employers, who are designated simply as "them." [...] As Kathy proceeds, however, the occupational discourse begins to give way to a more affective register.
>
> (Whitehead 2011, 59)

In the dystopic novel analyzed, Kathy's job as a carer for the state is eerie as she works for an industry (clone industry) that tries to alleviate the same suffering it creates. However, this difference aside, the situation of carers in *NLMG* is familiar in our societies in relation to the routinary "bureaucratized efficiency" (61). For example, Kathy expresses the contemporary concern about the fact that carers themselves may need to be taken care of due to the extenuating demands of the job. She explains the physical and psychological impact of caring, a job which requires both expertise and sympathy or compassion. This explains her vision that "carers aren't machines":

> You try and do your best for every donor, but in the end, it wears you down. You don't have unlimited patience and energy. So when you get a chance to choose, of course, you choose your own kind. That's natural. There's no way I could have gone on for as long as I have if I'd stopped

> feeling for my donors every step of the way [...] the work gets a lot harder when you don't have that deeper link with the donor.
>
> (Ishiguro 2006/2005, 4)

Feminist scholarship has also redefined the value of caring as fundamental due to the human dependence on the community and the necessity to relate, particularly when in need because of illness or disease. It challenges dominant visions of the subject as self-sufficient and in the pursuit of individualism. This relational paradigm conceives the act of caring as a new ethics:

> In contrast to an atomistic view of human nature, the ethics of care posits the image of a "relational self", a moral agent who is embedded in concrete relationships with others and who acquires a moral identity through interactive patterns of behaviour, perceptions and interpretations.
>
> (Parton 2003, 10).

As the quotation above shows, Kathy exemplifies such an ethic by stating the importance of relationality, which is expressed in the strong link between carer and donor. She also takes pride in her job affirming that "I'm a good carer" and that "it's important there are good carers" because "a good carer makes a big difference to what a donor's life's actually like" (Ishiguro 2006/2005, 76). Additionally, the novel destabilizes the barrier between such figures as Kathy will become a donor herself, in the same way that all human beings need to be taken care of at some point in their lives, for example, as we get old or sick. This reveals the futility of hierarchies and social distinctions. Yet, Kathy is well aware of the existence of social differences and takes sides, given that she prefers connecting with donors of her own kind, that is, her former friends and acquaintances. Besides, her childhood memories, which almost occupy the whole narrative, attest to her profound attachments and sensibility.

Although criticism has detected a certain passivity or resignation in accepting her fate and a lack of notorious rebellion on the part of all clone characters in general (Black 2009; De Villiers and Slabbert 2011; Garland-Thomson 2019; Lochner 2011; McDonald 2007; Toker and Chertoff 2008; Rosenfeld 2005), it is crucial not to forget the obvious and many impediments to sustained resistance. Not only the cultural and educational indoctrination have made the clones internalize their subaltern status and turn them into "docile bodies" (Benia 2019), but their short life-spam and diminishing health have not contributed to form a strong union against oppressive forces.

On the one hand, the curricular syllabus students receive at Hailsham, with a marked insistence on the values of duty and sacrifice promoted through the reading of Victorian literature, accounts for their submissiveness (Shaddox 2013). Furthermore, the presumed passivity has been intentionally depicted to show "the way most of us [...] accept our fate" (Ishiguro in Matthews 2009, 124).

When faced with the constant question about why they don't escape, Ishiguro postulates a very convincing argument, which is as if he put a mirror to us:

> I'm fascinated by the extent to which people don't run away and I think if you look around us, that is the remarkable fact, how much we accept what fate is giving us. Sometimes it's just passivity, sometimes it's just perspective. We don't have the perspective to think about running away.
>
> (Film Independent 2010)

This is an apt or feasible choice in that "the workings of biopolitical racism—the stratification of people into masters and servants—are as subtle and inescapable in Ishiguro's novel as they are in real life" (Kowalski 2014, 9).

On the other hand, even though Kathy feels attracted or belonging to her own community, this is fragile as in the 11 years (one-third of her life) that she has worked as a donor, she has lost most of them. In fact, "the only place to rebuild connection is in memories" since they gradually experience the loss of people and their home (Nazockdast and Ramin 2019, 109). Kathy ends up alone:

> It's like with my memories of Tommy and of Ruth. Once I'm able to have a quieter life, in whichever center they send me to, I'll have Hailsham with me, safely in my head, and that'll be something no one can take away.
>
> (Ishiguro 2006/2005, 281)

All in all, *NLMG* shows the growing dehumanization of medical science and progress, resorting to the irony that makes us better realize the eventual implications of our decisions and actions. The majority of the clones are not as "privileged" as the students raised at Hailsham but are merely "shadowy objects in test tubes" (256), and even Madame is aware of the anomalies in that system, detecting true signs of humanity in precisely those clones they so despise and pity. She envisions a more optimistic and humanist world when she remembers the scene of Kathy dancing to the song Baby, Never Let Me Go:

> I saw a new world coming rapidly. More scientific, efficient, yes. More cures for the old sicknesses. Very good. But a harsh, cruel world. And I saw a little girl, her eyes tightly closed, holding to her breast the old kind world, one that she knew in her heart could not remain, and she was holding it and pleading, never to let her go.
>
> (267)

Such "a new world" or the "old kind world" represents an alternative reality compared to the "harsh, cruel world" of the dystopia. Using memory has been identified as one key instrument for the rehumanization process enacted by Kathy, that is, as a way to form an identity by means of a first-person narrative

(Shaddox 2013). Furthermore, the relevance of affect and particularly the ethics of caring remains as the true egalitarian utopia that can reveal the nature of as well as alter the future of humanity.

Notes

1 Note the largely negative connotation of the word "guardian" for referring either to the legal custody of orphans or to the sense of property being controlled (Toker and Chertoff 2008, 167).

2 Feminists geographers have studied the so-called geographies of women's fear (Valentine 1989) arguing that, while based on factual high vulnerability, certain beliefs work well ideologically to prevent women from using public space (Pain 1993, 2001).

3 At 16 and as a transitional phase to the outside world, the students are temporarily sent to living facilities for young adult clones. Kathy, Tommy and Ruth are sent to the Cottages.

References

Aschroft, Bill, Gareth Griffins, and Helen Tiffins, eds. 1998. *Key Concepts in Postcolonial Studies*. New York: Routledge.

Black, Shameem. 2009. "Ishiguro's Inhuman Aesthetics." *MFS Modern Fiction Studies* 55.4: 785–807.

Benia, Safia. 2019. *Docile Bodies. Panopticism in Kazuo Ishiguro's Never Let Me Go*. PhD Diss. University of Mohamed Boudiaf-M'Sila.

Butler, Judith. 2022/2021. "Performative Acts and Gender Constitution: An Essay in Phenomenology and Feminist Theory." *Feminist Theory Reader: Local and Global Perspectives*, edited by Seung-Kyung Kim and Carole McCann, 353–361. New York: Routledge.

Cappo, Emily. 2009. *Repression and Displacement in Kazuo Ishiguro's When We Were Orphans and Never Let Me Go*. PhD Diss. University of Michigan.

Carroll, Rachel. 2010. "Imitations of Life: Cloning, Heterosexuality and the Human in Kazuo Ishiguro's *Never Let Me Go*." *Journal of Gender Studies* 19.1: 59–71.

De Villiers, Jan-Harm, and Magda Slabbert. 2011. "*Never Let Me Go*: Science Fiction and Legal Reality." *Literator: Journal of Literary Criticism, Comparative Linguistics and Literary Studies* 32.3: 85–103.

Du Bois, W. E. B, and Edwards Brent eds. 2007/1903. *The Souls of Black Folk*. Oxford: Oxford University Press.

Everett, Margaret. 2003. "The Social Life of Genes: Privacy, Property and the New Genetics." *Social Science & Medicine* 56.1: 53–65.

Ferrant, Gaëlle, Luca Maria Pesando, and Keiko Nowacka. 2014. "Unpaid Care Work: The Missing Link in the Analysis of Gender Gaps in Labour Outcomes." Boulogne Billancourt: OECD Development Center: 1–12.

Film Independent. 2010. "Kazuo Ishiguro Discusses his Intention Behind Writing the Novel *Never Let Me Go*." Available at: https://www.youtube.com/watch?v=_jCB59pPG7k&ab_channel=FilmIndependent

Folbre, Nancy, and Julie Nelson. 2000. "For Love or Money – or Both?" *Journal of Economic Perspectives* 14.4: 123–140.

Foucault, Michel. 2000/1975. *Vigilar y castigar: nacimiento de la prisión*. Buenos Aires: Siglo XXI.

Foucault, Michel. 2007/1976. *Historia de la sexualidad.* México, DF: Siglo XXI.

Garland-Thomson, Rosemarie. 2019. "World Building, Citizenship, and Disability: The Strange World of Kazuo Ishiguro's *Never Let Me Go.*" In *The Palgrave Handbook of Disability and Citizenship in the Global South*, 27–43. Cham: Palgrave Macmillan.

Gill, Josie. 2014. "Written on the Face: Race and Expression in Kazuo Ishiguro's *Never Let Me Go.*" *Modern Fiction Studies* 60.4: 844–862.

Goh, Robbie. 2011. "The Postclone-nial in Kazuo Ishiguro's *Never Let Me Go* and Amitav Ghosh's *The Calcutta Chromosome*: Science and the Body in the Asian Diaspora." *Ariel: A Review of International English Literature* 41.3–4: 45–71.

Guo, Wen. 2015. "Human Cloning as the Other in Ishiguro's *Never Let Me Go.*" *CLCWeb: Comparative Literature and Culture* 17.5: 1–7.

Hall, Stuart. 1987. "Minimal Selves." In *Identity: The Real Me*, edited by Homi Bhabha and Lisa Appignanesi, 175–215. London: Institute of Contemporary Arts.

Hall, Stuart. 1998. "Cultural Identity and Diaspora." In *Community, Culture, Difference*, edited by John Rutherford, 222–237. London: Lawrence & Wishart.

Hawley, John Charles, and Emmanuel Nelson, eds. 2001. *Encyclopedia of Postcolonial Studies*. Greenwood Publishing Group.

Himmelweit, Susan, and Ania Plomien. 2014. "Feminist Perspectives on Care: Theory, Practice and Policy." In *The SAGE Handbook of Feminist Theory*, edited by M. Evans, C. Hemmings, M. Henry, H. Johnstone, S. Madhok, A. Plomien, and S. Wearing, 446–464. London: Sage.

Huxley, Aldous. 1932. *Brave New World.* New York: Harper & Brothers.

Hyvärinen, Matti. 2008. "Friendship, Care, and Politics: Kazuo Ishiguro's *Never Let Me Go.*" *Redescriptions: Political Thought, Conceptual History and Feminist Theory* 12.1: 202–223.

Ikas, Karin. 2017. "Slavery and Resilience in Caryl Phillips's Novel Cambridge." In *Postcolonial Justice*, edited by Anke Bartels, Lars Eckstein, and Nicole Wall, 217–243. Leiden: Brill.

Ishiguro, Kazuo. 2006/2005. *Never Let Me Go.* Kent: Faber and Faber.

Kowalski, Andrea. 2014. "How to Create Inhumanity: Kazuo Ishiguro's *Never Let Me Go.*" *Verso: An Undergraduate Journal of Literary Criticism* 9–21. https://ojs.library.dal.ca/verso/issue/archive

Lochner, Liani. 2011. "'This is what we're Supposed to be Doing, Isn't it?': Scientific Discourse in Kazuo Ishiguro's *Never Let Me Go*". In *Kazuo Ishiguro: New Critical Visions of the Novels*, edited by Sebastian Groes and Barry Lewis, 225–236. London: Red Globe Press.

Matthews, Sean. 2009. "I'm Sorry I Can't Say More. An Interview with Kazuo Ishiguro." In *Kazuo Ishiguro: Contemporary Critical Perspectives*, edited by Sean Matthews and Sebastian Groes, 114–126. New York: Continuum.

McDonald, Keith. 2007: "Days of Past Futures: Kazuo Ishiguro's *Never Let Me Go* as 'Speculative Memoir'." *Biography* 30.1: 74–83.

McLeod, John. 2000. *Beginning Postcolonialism.* Manchester: Manchester University Press.

Nazockdast, Sara, and Zohreh Ramin. 2019. "The Copy and the Real: Language-Games of Personhood in Ishiguro's *Never Let Me Go.*" *International Journal of English Language & Translation Studies* 7.4: 99–110.

Pain, Rachel. 1993. Crime, *Social Control and Spatial Constraint: a Study of Women's Fear of Sexual Violence*. PhD Diss. University of Edinburgh.

Pain, Rachel. 2001. "Gender, Race, Age and Fear in the City." *Urban Studies* 38.5–6: 899–913.

Parton, Nigel. 2003. "Rethinking Professional Practice: The Contributions of Social Constructionism and the Feminist 'Ethics of Care'." *British Journal of Social Work* 33.1:1–16.

Quabeck, Franziska. 2017. "Cultural Rights and the Politics of Recognition in Kazuo Ishiguro's *Never Let Me Go.*" In *Diaspora, Law and Literature*, edited by Klaus Stierstorfer and Daniela Carpi, 205–222. Berlin: De Gruyter.

Robbins, Bruce. 2007. "Caring: Kazuo Ishiguro's *Never Let Me* Go". In *Upward Mobility and the Common Good:* Toward a Literary History of the Welfare State, 199–210. Princeton: Princeton University Press.

Rosenfeld, Aaron S. 2005. "Re-membering the Future: Doris Lessing's 'Experiment in Autobiography'." *Critical Survey* 17.1: 40–55.

Sevenhuijsen, Selma. 2003. *Citizenship and the Ethics of Care: Feminist Considerations on Justice, Morality and Politics.* New York: Routledge.

Shaddox, Karl. 2013. "Generic Considerations in Ishiguro's *Never Let Me Go.*" *Human Rights Quarterly* 35.2: 448–469.

Snaza, Nathan. 2015. "The Failure of Humanizing Education in Kazuo Ishiguro's *Never Let Me Go.*" *Lit: Literature Interpretation Theory* 26.3: 215–234.

Sibley, David. 2002. *Geographies of Exclusion: Society and Difference in the West.* New York: Routledge.

Stacy, Ivan. 2015. "Complicity in Dystopia: Failures of Witnessing in China Miéville's *The City and the City* and Kazuo Ishiguro's *Never Let Me Go.*" *Partial Answers: Journal of Literature and the History of Ideas* 13.2: 225–250.

Steinberg, Deborah. 1997. *Bodies in Glass: Genetics, Eugenics, Embryo Ethics.* Manchester: Manchester University Press.

Toker, Leona, and Daniel Chertoff. 2008. "Reader Response and the Recycling of Topoi in Kazuo Ishiguro's *Never Let Me Go.*" *Partial Answers: Journal of Literature and the History of Ideas* 6.1: 163–180.

Valentine, Gill. 1989. "The Geography of Women's Fear." *Area* 21.4: 385–390.

Vichiensing, Matava. 2017. "The othering in Kazuo Ishiguro's *Never Let Me Go.*" *Advances in Language and Literary Studies* 8.4: 126–135.

Walkovitz, Rebecca. 2007. "Unimaginable Largeness: Kazuo Ishiguro, Translation, and the New World Literature". *Novel: A Forum on Fiction* 40.3: 216–239.

Whitehead, Anne. 2011. "Writing with Care: Kazuo Ishiguro's *Never Let Me Go.*" *Contemporary Literature* 52.1: 54–83.

2 Ecocriticism

"Environmental Dystopias" and the Post-Pastoral

Unsettling Environments in Environmental Dystopianism

Science fiction literature, film and scholarship have often focused on the urban space (Maurer and Koren-Kuik 2018; Sobchack 1988), which seems to be a privileged *topos* to present dramatic events affecting a large population. The highly changing nature of the city is identified as an apt metaphor for the reflection of posthuman subjectivities (Barros-Grela 2018; Orbaugh 2006). However, in *Never Let Me Go* (*NLMG*) it is the remote and rural places that are chosen to reflect the population control most commonly found in urban cityscapes (Cannella 2017).

Ishiguro's novel features an "unsettling environment" (Lilley 2016): "What at first seems like an account of childhood in an idyllic country boarding house turns out to be sinister and profoundly troubling, a book that questions at the deepest level what it is to be human" (Dewan 2019, 95). Critics have remarked that it alters the type of setting expected in dystopias, which tend to develop not only in cities but also portray grim environments as a reflection of the decaying world therein portrayed: "*Never Let Me Go* is set in the sleepy English countryside, its pastoral setting sharply contrasting with the bleak, clinical morality behind the novel's premise" (Rosenfeld 2021, 113). Lisa Musial also agrees that, in relation to the "pastoral visions of the English countryside", "this distinct setting creates a stark contrast to the characters' harsh reality" (2018, 57).

The use of the pastoral is frequent in British literary tradition,[1] although Ishiguro complicates or actualizes the well-known genre by incorporating a different perspective, the so-called post-pastoral and ecocriticism (Lilley 2016; Musial 2018). Following Garrard, "the ambivalence of pastoral will not be eliminated but enhanced by ecocritical readings" (2012, 62). The analysis of such settings and scenarios is paramount as they do not appear as mere "context" or "background" to the action; rather Kathy's recollections from Hailsham, the Cottages and other counties in England are generally linked to the corresponding natural environments (Lilley 2016). This perspective reflects a critical understanding of landscape in contemporary cultural geography not as "an objective set of forms"

DOI: 10.4324/9781003530695-3

but as a "signifying system" whose meaning is (re)constructed by each individual or the "perceiver–observer" (dell'Agnese and Amilhat-Szary 2015, 4).

Hailsham and Beyond: Discovering (the Limits of) a "Phantasy Land"

The characters' sense of place and geographical knowledge are not only very imperfect or limited but necessarily idealized. As they admit: "any place beyond Hailsham was like a fantasy land; we had only the haziest notions of the world outside and about what was and wasn't possible there" (Ishiguro 2006/2005, 66).

First, an important element that creates such a pastoral scenario is the very school Hailsham, also referred to as the students' house and a "privileged estate" (4), which "is located in a peaceful setting, sheltered in 'a smooth hollow with fields rising on all sides' [and] is reminiscent of an idyllic Renaissance country-house" (57). The surrounding nature is generally described as calm and features harmonious images which are typically bucolic such as "shrubs and flowerbeds" (34) or the pond "laying] to the south of the house [where] you'd find a tranquil atmosphere waiting, with ducks and bulrushes and pond-weed" (25). Some other places are also associated with romanticized sketches and the idea to break free from routine activity or "civilized" society:

> We loved our sports pavilion, maybe because it reminded us of those sweet little cottages people always had in picture books when we were young. I can remember us back in the Juniors, pleading with guardians to hold the next lesson in the pavilion instead of the usual room. Then by the time we were in Senior 2—when we were twelve, going on thirteen—the pavilion had become the place to hide out with your best friends when you wanted to get away from the rest of Hailsham. [...] ideally you and your friends wanted the place just to yourselves [...] The guardians were always telling us to be civilized about it, but in practice, you needed to have some strong personalities in your group to stand a chance of getting the pavilion during a break or free period.
>
> (5–6)

Musial argues that *NLMG* "appears very calm regarding its dystopian elements and shows subtle contrasts rather than harsh realities" (2018, 59). This means that the existence of "unpleasant realities" is notably downplayed such us by the use of euphemisms (completing instead of dying in relation to organ donation) and other indirect or imprecise allusions: "Descriptions of nature are not harsh, the only sign alluding to an unpleasant reality are the dark woods surrounding Hailsham, in which people allegedly disappear" (59). At the same time, however, both Hailsham itself and the closest natural surroundings are characterized by an uneasy sense of control. According to Cannella

(2017, 94–5), the school's "panoptic physical structure" extends well into the physical spaces students seem to enjoy.[2] Thus, they cannot sometimes go wherever they please: "if there were no guardians around, you could take a short cut through the rhubarb patch" (Ishiguro 2006/2005, 25). Or, in relation to the pond, students may feel relaxed but also really surveyed there:

> It wasn't, though, a good place for a discrete conversation—not nearly as good as the lunch queue. For a start you could be clearly seen from the house. And the way the sound travelled across the water was hard to predict; if people wanted to eavesdrop, it was the easiest thing to walk down the outer path and crouch in the bushes on the other side of the pond.
>
> (25)

Cannella rightly notes some signs of the students' critical awareness of the subtle power exerted over them in that they "can identify a picturesque pond and clearing as a threat to their privacy and have to covertly communicate in the lunch line" (2017, 95). However, this crucial awareness often appears minimized and the memories of these places are idealized for the most part. At first sight, the main reason behind the representation of an idealized landscape is that it functions as a haven for the equally idealized childhood which is evoked in the novel. Musial notes that

> the place's pastoral notion is underlined by Kathy's memories of it as an adult and carer for donors [given that] seeing images of nature often reminds her of Hailsham [...] Kathy's memories of Hailsham are often described as nostalgic, which too is one of the main characteristics of the pastoral.
>
> (2018, 57–8)

For Deborah Lilley, Hailsham needs to be understood more in cultural than geographical terms, the nature of which has been (re)constructed or distorted by the imagination:

> it comes to be understood as less a place in itself than a particular way of looking at place. When Kathy and Tommy are finally confronted with a photograph of Hailsham towards the end of the novel, it is not recognized as the place they recall: [...] In this way, the novel calls our attention towards pastoral ways of looking, highlighting the selectivity by which it operates, and the effects that it produces. For Kathy and Tommy, the pastoral represents a desire for consolation and escapism that cannot be realized, one that fails to mesh with the realities of the material or cultural landscapes of the novel: there is no "place" for the clones beyond Hailsham.
>
> (2016, 68)

Similarly, David Gurnham, who examines the role of the imagination and memory in the novel, as well as the role of nostalgia in science fiction in general, alludes to the "inadequacy" and "unreliability" of the students' memories of Hailsham, concluding that it actually "never existed outside its collective imagination" (2016, 198–9).

In turn, the students' experience and understanding of nature are also shaped by the instruction received at Hailsham, which shows a pastoral influence in the collection of postcards of rural England. The charming and traditional descriptions used in the geography lessons they receive anticipate, and somehow replace, their encounter with the actual settings:

> There'd be little villages with streams going through them, white monuments on hillsides, old churches beside fields; if she [Miss Emily] was telling us about a coastal place, there'd be beaches crowded with people, cliffs with seagulls. I suppose she wanted us to have a grasp of what was out there surrounding us, and it's amazing, even now, after all these miles I've covered as a carer, the extent to which my idea of the various counties is still set by these pictures Miss Emily put up on her easel. I'd be driving through Derbyshire, say, and catch myself looking for a particular village green with a mock-Tudor pub and a war memorial—and realize it's the image Miss Emily showed us the first time I ever heard of Derbyshire.
> (Ishiguro 2006/2005, 64–5)

This idealization is more or less openly recognized in the novel, often through the strategy of using a different temporal framework that explains or justifies the (obvious) difference. For example, by such an allusion to the actual photograph of Hailsham which characters cannot recognize in late life. The simple fact that it reflects "just a bit of countryside" does not match with their memory of the place (244). Or by the illusion, after leaving Hailsham for the Cottages,[3] of glimpsing places that they think could be Hailsham but turn out to be phantasmagoric, and here the landscape described is "oddly crooked" and "gives you the creeps" (116).

Yet, another key function of using such a simplified and flawless portrayal of the world through the pastoral is to conceal the existence and atrocities of the cloning system. Following Lilley,

> its bucolic idyll also sequesters the living reality of the cloning technology that supports and shames the world outside its fences [....] The limited view of Hailsham initially given through pastoral's selective lens is paralleled by the blinkered perspective that the place affords its students.
> (2016, 64)

This explains that the characters' pastoral visions clash against the dystopian reality.

However, Lilley adds that the use of the pastoral is not completely antithetic to the expression of catastrophe and barbarism, in view of growing representations found in contemporary writing which show "pastoral's adaptability to various contexts and its receptivity to interaction with different forms" (62). In fact, the conventions of the genre may well have been modified, which is shown in how Ishiguro adapts the (anti)pastoral to reflect an "anti-utopian" reality (Chatterjee 2019). Accordingly, Ishiguro's novel can be interpreted in relation to the emerging movement of British writers who are engaged with a new awareness about our relation to nature or, taking Peter Boxall's label, "environmental dystopianism" (2013, 217). Using also Charles Martindale's concept of "green politics" (1997, 119), Lilley shows how *NLMG* reflects the "ambivalence" of the pastoral as "both 'green' and 'political', at once 'aesthetic', 'critical', 'escapist', and 'selective'" (2016, 63).

For this reason, the novel has been analyzed from a post-pastoral approach, given the way in which it incorporates the pastoral but also shows a respectful relation regarding nature which breaks the distance with human action. This is an apt framework to reflect also on the condition of the clones since the exploitation of nature has been equated with the abuse of groups traditionally marginalized, as ecofeminism has notably studied out of the traditional association of women with the natural world. In this case, the clones are equated with marginal people or disposable rubbish, at the hands of human exploitation or consumption. For example, as already seen in the previous chapter, this is how Ruth conceives her own origins out of the social mistreatment she experiments: "We're modelled from *trash*. Junkies, prostitutes, winos, tramps. Convicts, maybe, just so long as they aren't psychos. That's what we come from" (Ishiguro 2006/2005, 164; emphasis original).

The existence of the clones reflects the ongoing generation of minorities, which exposes the human power exerted over nature and other beings, in this case through biotechnology:

> The post-pastoral conscience wants to overcome these oppressions and empower nature as well as people [...] *Never Let Me Go* rather subverts this by presenting the exploitation of the clones seeking solace in nature. They do benefit from their peaceful surroundings, which they meet with respect. As they cannot be placed in either the human or nature category, they complicate traditional mechanisms of oppression. Thus, the novel extends the post-pastoral by focusing on the treatment of a newly emerged, artificially created minority.
>
> (Musial 2018, 60–1)

Borrowing from ecocriticism, the novel has been categorized as an *ecobildungsroman* by taking into account the environmental aspects of the text as well as the main focus on its nonhuman agents. In fact, the combined study of place and identity is relevant in contemporary criticism ever since the so-called spatial turn, since the two categories are inextricably linked, only that in this case the former constitutes "an active force in the development of the nonhuman" (Atherton 2018, 2). In other words, as also argued by posthumanist theory (Matek and Pataki 2020), (eco)critical readings of the novel move away from traditional anthropocentric approaches that exclude both the clones and nature.

Together with this rejection or criticism of the human, which is concomitant to many dystopian science fiction texts,[4] the genre presents a marked attention to the environment, generally the urban, or rather post-urban, setting which explains or fosters the development of posthuman identity, opening a new paradigm of "post-human spatialities" (Barros-Grela 2018, 28). In Ishiguro's novel, posthuman representations offer a further innovative perspective as they center on the more peripheral rural spaces.

At the same time, it equally shares similar tenets of environmentalism in the science fiction such as the concern for climatic crisis and more particularly the effects of human action upon the environment. Humanity's negative impact in terms of planetary destruction or the damage inflicted upon the natural world, including our own survival as a species, has long been present in the genre. For this reason, *NLMG* can well be read as a "anthroposcenic narrative" in that it "demarcate[s] the extinction of utopian possibility in visceral terms, as a result of our exploitation of Earth's environment" (Hay 2021, 11).

In the novel, the clones are equated to the discarded waste generated by human consumption and which pollutes the Earth. For example, in the last scene of the novel Kathy is looking at a desolate field which is almost empty ("the cluster of three or four trees above me were the only things breaking the wind for miles)" except for different signs of waste (Ishiguro 2006/2005, 282); she initially observes how "all sorts of rubbish had caught and tangled" around a barbed wire and continues with other images of abandonment affecting the planet: "It was like the debris you get on a seashore […] Up in the branches of the trees, too, I could see, flapping about, torn plastic sheeting and bits of old carrier bags" (282). She then believes this dismal ending represents the destiny of her own life: "I half-closed my eyes and imagined this was the spot where everything I'd ever lost since my childhood had washed up" (282). In addition, Ruth, apart from associating her own origins with trash, has a dream in which she envisions a landscape and accumulated rubbish floating around: "I was looking out of the window and everything outside was flooded. Just like a giant lake. And I could see rubbish floating by under my window, empty drinks cartons, everything" (221). These comparisons show how "they have been turned into tradable disposable bodies, inscribed in a global market of post-anthropocentric exploitation" (Braidotti 2013, 70).

Furthermore, the gradual detachment from the environment and living things is a common reflection of their feelings of isolation and radical exclusion from any natural or human interaction. For example, the narrative becomes more and more sinister as Kathy becomes a donor and lives mostly in solitude wandering between the gloomy facilities for those about to die and the vast landscape:

> the recovery centers she visits are reduced to a single room, where, alienated and unhappy, she spends the time with dying clones. When she rushes from one center to another, commuting between Dover, Kingsfield or Norfolk, as her presence is required by different donors, she has only "the roads, the big grey sky and my daydreams for company" (204). Exhausted, facing pain and death, Kathy can no longer establish a harmonious relationship with the surrounding environment. Although she travels a lot now, she remains completely cut off from the "normal" world. She knows that the cruel, violent, inhuman environment in which she is forced to live can only bring about death.
>
> (Brînzeu 2011, 94)

This explains why Kathy, in turn, rejects the world and retreats instead into the inner reality of her thoughts and memories, which become an important means of survival and self-definition, as it will be shown in the final chapter.

In conclusion, the portrayal of place in general and nature, in particular, is strongly linked to the clones' identity in Ishiguro's environmental dystopia, suggesting how the themes of degradation and exploitation loom behind an apparently naïve and pastoral setting. This turns out to be a façade of the atrocities that await the clones. As a result, as they grow up and leave their "secure" confines, they soon learn that the world beyond Hailsham is no fairyland and has certain boundaries for them too. Initially, they leave Hailsham for the Cottages, which are the "pre-donation centers" (Lee 2019, 272) or, as Aaron Rosenfeld states, not an "idyll" but a "Limbo" (2021, 136) before their due destiny is realized. Finally, Kelly Rich (2015) has studied the material environment the clones inhabit or temporally occupy by paying attention to other infrastructures, such as the recovery centers and hospitals, which reveal their preordained existence and therefore limits of the world they are allowed to know.

Notes

1 The English national identity is very much shaped by idealized country landscapes, which is proved in the manifold literary evocations of an "earlier and happier rural England" (Williams 1973, 35). Furthermore, this idealized English landscape, which is represented as "bucolic", "picturesque" and "tidy", reflects not only a national inclination but particularly the preferred taste of the upper classes (Lowenthal and Prince 1965, 186, 190, 219). Yet, note also recent revisions of the pastoral from an ecocritical approach which see traditional texts in this literature (Virgil, Petrarch and Milton, among others) as an early manifestation of environmental concerns such as pollution or deforestation (Hiltner 2011).

2 She actually continues to argue for the presence of an intricate web of surveillance which insinuates further control of both guardians and students may be at a regional and national level:

> the panoptic mechanism that Ishiguro constructs in his novel is not limited to Hailsham and its grounds. Hailsham itself is situated in a way that allows for the institution to fall subject to constant supervision and submission, placing this panoptic institution within an even larger panoptic mechanism [...] While Hailsham is panoptic for its students, it is simultaneously subject to a more obscure panopticon. (102)

3 Hailsham students are transferred to the Cottages where they will learn their role as carers for donors first and then in preparation for their own eventual donations.

4 Especially with the revolutions brought by biotechnology and digitalization, most fictions jungle between the depiction of the fears of an apocalyptic world, including the end of humanity, and "the new possibilities in terms of species evolution and mutation towards the post-human" (Machinal 2016, n.p.). In this respect, normally texts have represented the figure of the "extreme, wholly other posthuman", which creates anxiety and is generated as a critique of technology, but there have also emerged other resilient and more optimistic representations around the "hybrid posthuman", which "retains a very familiar 'natural self' and is an extension of rather than 'successor' to the human being" (Seaman 2007, 259).

References

Atherton, Hannah Mae. 2018. *The Art of Ecological Selfing: Speculative Ecobildungsromane in Cloud Atlas and Never Let Me Go*. MA Thesis. Georgetown University.

Barros-Grela, Eduardo. 2018. "Past Future Cityscapes: Narratives of the Post-Human in Post-Urban Environments." In *Cityscapes of the Future: Urban Spaces in Science Fiction*, edited by Yael Maurer and Meyrav Koren-Kuik, 28–48. Leiden: Brill.

Boxall, Peter. 2013. *Twenty-First-Century Fiction: A Critical Introduction*. Cambridge: Cambridge University Press.

Braidotti, Rosi. 2013. *The Posthuman*. Malden: Polity.

Brînzeu, Pia. 2011. "'All Over the Country': Cloned Spaces in Kazuo Ishiguro's *Never Let Me Go*." *BAS British and American Studies* 17: 91–100.

Cannella, Megan. 2017. "Unreliable Physical Places and Memories as Posthuman Narration in Ishiguro's *Never Let Me Go*." *Sanglap: Journal of Literary and Cultural Inquiry* 3.2: 92–126.

Chatterjee, Arnab. 2019. "Exploring an Anti-Utopian Subtext in Kazuo Ishiguro's *Never Let Me Go*." *Interdisciplinary Literary Studies* 21.2: 109–124.

Dell'Agnese, Elena, and Anne-Laure Amilhat-Szary. 2015. "Borderscapes: From Border Landscapes to Border Aesthetics." *Geopolitics* 20: 1–10

Dewan, Motikala Subba. 2019. "Paradox Between Religion and Biotechnology in Ishiguro's *Never Let Me Go*." *Bon Voyage* 4.1: 95–104.

Garrard, Greg. 2012. *Ecocriticism*. 2nd ed. London: Routledge.

Gurnham, David. 2016. *Memory, Imagination, Justice: Intersections of Law and Literature*. London: Routledge

Hay, Jonathan. 2021. "Utopia's Extinction: The Anthroposcenic Landscapes of Ursula K. Le Guin." *Messengers from the Stars: On Science Fiction and Fantasy* 5.1: 10–27.

Hiltner, Ken. 2011. *What Else Is Pastoral? Renaissance Literature and the Environment*. Ithaca: Cornell University Press.

Ishiguro, Kazuo. 2006/2005. *Never Let Me Go*. Kent: Faber and Faber.

Lee, Ji Eun. 2019. "Norfolk and the Sense of Loss: The Bildungsroman and Colonial Subjectivity in Kazuo Ishiguro's *Never Let Me Go*." *Texas Studies in Literature and Language* 61.3: 270–290.

Lilley, Deborah. 2016. "Unsettling Environments: New Pastorals in Kazuo Ishiguro's *Never Let Me Go* and Sarah Hall's *The Carhullan Army*." *Green Letters* 20.1: 60–71.

Lowenthal, David, and Hugh Prince. 1965. "English Landscape Tastes." *Geographical Review* 55.2: 186–222.

Machinal, Hélène. 2016. "Devenirs de l'humain et fiction contemporaine: imaginaires de la fin, corps bio-technologiques et subjectivités numériques." *Études britanniques contemporaines* 50: n.p.

Martindale, Charles, ed. 1997. *The Cambridge Companion to Virgil*. Cambridge: Cambridge University Press.

Matek, Ljubica, and Jelena Pataki. 2020. Kazuo Ishiguro's *Never Let Me Go* as a Posthumanist Dystopia. In *Essays in Honour of Boris Berić's Sixty-Fifth Birthday: "What's Past Is Prologue"*, edited by Gabrijela Buljan et al., 3–20. Newcastle: Cambridge Scholars Publishing.

Maurer, Yael, and Meyrav Koren-Kuik. 2018. *Cityscapes of the Future: Urban Spaces in Science Fiction*. Leiden: Brill.

McDonald, Keith. 2007. "Days of Past Futures: Kazuo Ishiguro's *Never Let Me Go* as 'Speculative Memoir'." *Biography* 30.1: 74–83.

Musial, Lisa. 2018. "A Landscape Lullaby? The Function of (Post-) Pastoral Elements in Kazuo Ishiguro's *Never Let Me Go*." *Satura* 1: 56–62.

Orbaugh, Sharalyn. 2006. "Frankenstein and the Cyborg Metropolis: The Evolution of Body and City in Science Fiction Narratives." In *Cinema Anime: Critical Engagement with Japanese Animations*, edited by Steven Brown, 81–111. New York: Palgrave Macmillan.

Rich, Kelly. 2015. "'Look in the Gutter': Infrastructural Interiority in *Never Let Me Go*." *Modern Fiction Studies* 61.4: 631–561.

Rosenfeld, Aaron. 2021. "Dystopia and the End of Character in Zamyatin, Burgess, and Ishiguro." In *Character and Dystopia: The Last Men*, 112–148. New York: Routledge.

Seaman, Myra. 2007. "Becoming More (than) Human: Affective Posthumanisms, Past and Future." *Journal of Narrative Theory* 37.2: 246–275.

Sobchack, Vivian. 1988. "Cities on the Edge of Time: The Urban Science Fiction Film." *East-West: Film Journal* 3.1: 4–20.

Williams, Raymond. 1973. *The Country and the City*. New York: Oxford University Press.

3 Looking for Hope

The Role of Love and Art, and Other Religious Undertones of Redemption

NLMG has been labeled as "a mild and melancholy dystopia" (Toker and Chertoff 2008, 163) due to that general elegiac tone which is explained and becomes intensified in the culmination of the text when Kathy mourns the loss of her past and loved-ones as well as seems to lose all hope and accept her tragic destiny:

> I half-closed my eyes and imagined that this was the spot where everything I'd lost since my childhood had washed up, and I was now standing in front of it, and if I waited long enough, a tiny figure on the horizon would appear across the field, and gradually get larger until I could see Tommy, and he'd wave, maybe even call. The fantasy never got beyond that—I didn't let it—and though the tears rolled down my cheeks, I wasn't sobbing or out of control. I just waited for a bit, then turned back to the car, to drive off wherever I was supposed to be.
>
> (Ishiguro 2006/2005, 282)

As it will be shown along the chapter, this interpretation of "the poignant melancholy of the novel's ending" (Toker and Chertoff 2008, 174) perfectly captures one of the reasons why the novel is certainly different from other dystopias.

Despite common beliefs about the genre being "bleak" or "depressing" and the dominant representations in some of the most classic dystopian texts, in "The Persistence of Hope in Dystopian Science Fiction" Raffaela Baccolini also argues that "utopia is maintained in dystopia" (2004, 520). In fact, Ishiguro's novel can be read in light of contemporary writing that has shifted the focus from fixed plots with a purely catastrophist message toward more open stories where there is also room for hope. Thus, apart from the traditional "dark" societies and scenarios incorporating necessary warnings against the future, hope is an essential element in these narratives for being understood as "an expression of struggle and resistance" (520). The important role of hope can be analyzed

DOI: 10.4324/9781003530695-4

through the representation of love, the most important theme apart from cloning, to which it actually displaces:

> The novel is thus about the triumph of emotion against the cold scientific and clinical backdrop in which the clones are raized, indeed they are brought up and taught not to feel and love but against these odds it is precisely these feelings that Tommy and Kathy experience. *Never Let me Go* is thus a story about the utopian quest for love in a deeply dystopian environment which contrives to their annihilation in speculative England. (Ching Yi 2016, 35)

Besides the power of love to transform the students' lives, art and religion also appear as key utopian spaces such as for developing individuals' identity outside society's constrictions or finding salvation.

Something to Go On: Deferrals

First, the idea of redemption in the novel is best shown in how the characters believe that their life expectancy can be extended if they prove to be in love. Besides this explicit comparison, love is generally understood as an act of (free) will and resistance to one's destiny or external authority, thus representing a mighty tool for hope in the hands of young people who are believed to have no power over themselves.

Against the terrifying background of cloning, the novel centers on the ordinary lives of young students who, living together and having each other as only family, develop strong bonds of friendship and love. Kathy and Tommy are inseparable friends and confidants and, as they grow up, there are also situations in which a love relationship is insinuated such as when Tommy and Ruth break up for the first time and Kathy is rumored to be "Ruth's natural successor" (Ishiguro 2006/2005, 115). Yet Ruth persuades Kathy herself to help her get Tommy back. Only 11 years later Kathy and Tommy get together as a couple, after they have left Hailsham and grown more apart. However, they still feel as if no time has passed between them and start a relationship at a crucial moment of their lives: Tommy has undergone two donations, and Kathy is ending her career as a carer before she also becomes a donor.

The subject of love not only is central in the love triangle formed by Kathy, Tommy and Ruth but also emerges as an instrument that can give students hope against their fate, which is shown in Kathy's gradual transition to believe in the so-called deferrals. As rumor has it, students from Hailsham can get deferrals, that is, they are able to postpone their donations (and therefore extend their lives) for a few years, although this option is only available to students who are truly in love. Couples are given some extra time to stay together "so long as [they] *qualified*!", which means they have to "convince" their tutors by showing some evidence of their love (Ishiguro 2006/2005, 150; emphasis original). Tommy becomes particularly intrigued and starts theorizing about this "special arrangement", coming up with the hypothesis that the Art Gallery was the means by which students could show if their love was genuine rather than only a "sex thing" or a "stupid crush" (173–4):

> there has to be a way to judge if they're really telling the truth. That they aren't just saying they're in love, just to defer their donations. You see how difficult it could be to decide? [...] But the point is, whoever decides, Madame or whoever it is, *they need something to go on.* [...] Madame's got a gallery somewhere filled with stuff by students from when they were tiny. Suppose two people come up and say they're in love. She can find the art they've done over years and years. She can see if they go. If they match. Don't forget, Kath, what she's got reveals our souls.
>
> (173; emphasis original)

It looks like students themselves have *something to go on* too and start considering this new even if ephemeral hope. Tommy appears interested as he is in a couple with Ruth and thinks that she "believes it all" and will want to "take it further" (ask for a deferral) at some point (175). Kathy is initially cautious due to the difficulty of the search as they do not know how to "apply" and what they are "supposed to do" (177), and Tommy also acknowledges that they are rather lost as "it's probably not just Madame that decides. There's probably people higher up than her, people who never set foot in Hailsham" (175). However, he also persuades Kathy into giving it a chance: "there's only one obvious way forward. And that's to find Madame" (177). This is why he seems to invest his time in art rather than any other love expression. In his enthusiasm, he even confesses to Kathy that he has been drawing secretly (not even Ruth knows) "his imaginary animals", which he considers quite worthy even though his former pictures were never considered good enough to go into the Gallery: "Honest, Kath, it's nothing like anything I ever did at Hailsham" (175).

Eventually, it is Kathy and Tommy who ask for a deferral and it is Ruth who encourages that as she is about to die and regrets that she deliberately prevented Kathy and Tommy from discovering their mutual love when they were students:

> It should have been you two. I'm not pretending I didn't always see that. Of course I did, as far back as I can remember. But I kept you apart. [...] You and Tommy, you've got to try and get a deferral. If it's you two, there's got to be a chance. A real chance.
>
> (228)

Although Kathy contemplates that "it is too late" as Tommy has already undergone his second donation, when she becomes her carer, they start "a new phase together" (233). Rather, they resume their former or interrupted friendship/love relationship even if with a different maturity and the practice of sex:

> Their relationship at the time is almost idyllic, in spite of having to waste their time together in the recovery center. They spend time reading and talking [...] as if all the years melted away; the only thing that changed about their relationship is that they finally start being intimate. [...] They are still aware of the reality that they have only limited and insufficient time together, therefore they decide to explore the rumor about the deferrals of the donations for couples.
>
> (Mašínová 2016, 57)

It is Kathy herself who initiates the sexual relationship, which she considers as a proper sign of "intimacy" in a couple (Ishiguro 2006/2005, 234), for no other reason indeed that the fact that the mysterious option of deferral still lingers in her mind since Ruth's proposal. She is very concerned about the passing of time and the imminence of Tommy's particular death:

> we hardly brought up Madame or that conversation with Ruth in the car that day. But the very fact of my having become his carer served as a reminder that we weren't there to mark time. And so too, of course, did Tommy's animal drawings.
>
> (235)

For this reason, Tommy is also pressed to improve his art, which is why he asks her an opinion about it:

> But I was aware too why the animals had emerged again, and of all the possible layers behind Tommy's apparently casual query. At the least, I could see, he was showing me he hadn't forgotten, even though we'd hardly discussed anything openly; he was telling me he wasn't complacent, and that he was busy getting on with his part of the preparations.
>
> (237)

Having Madame's address from their last conversation with Ruth, Kathy and Tommy confront the art collector with a firm conviction about their request: "we know you must get tired of it, all these couples coming to you, claiming to be in love. Tommy and me, we never would have come and bothered you if we weren't really sure" (247). However, they discover that their hopes about deferrals are futile given that their artwork serves a different purpose than they thought. There they also meet Miss Emily, the head guardian, who in one of her customary speeches finally reveals the truth about the clones' future, which she had tried to conceal from the students so far. She coldly confesses that they let rumors or lies spread despite knowing the potential damage that it could entail for those who were hopeful. Besides, she dismisses students' beliefs and expectations as a simple illusion:

> [Madame] Marie-Claude never did worry about it. Her view was: 'If they're so foolish, let them believe it.' [...] After many years of it, I came not exactly to the same viewpoint. But I began to think, well, perhaps I shouldn't worry. It's not my doing, after all. And for the few couples who get disappointed, the rest will never put it to the test anyway. It's something for them to dream about, a little fantasy. What harm is there? But for the two of you, I can see this doesn't apply. You are serious. You've thought carefully. You've *hoped* carefully. For students like you, I do feel regret. It gives me no pleasure at all to disappoint you. But there it is.
>
> (253; emphasis original)

Miss Emily continues to explain then why the revelation of their souls through art was not interpreted as a proof of love. Rather it was a way to "*prove [they] had souls at all*" in an attempt to mend the clones' conditions in the eyes of society (254; emphasis original), given that outside Hailsham students are "reared in deplorable conditions" (255). Together with Madame, the co-founder of that social experiment or "little movement" (258) of institutions like Hailsham, Miss Emily advocates that clones were treated in a "more humane and better way" (253), but just until they donate as it turns out. In other words, despite the supposed well-intended motivations of some reformers like Madame and Miss Emily, the students learn that the practice of cloning is never put in question and so their tragic destiny remains essentially the same:

> you were kept away from the worst of those horrors. We were able to do that much for you at least. But this dream of yours, this dream of being able to *defer*. Such a thing would always have been beyond us to grant, even at the height of our influence.
>
> (256; italics original)

Moreover, quite ironically, even though Miss Emily complains that society no longer treats the clones with the dignity once offered in Hailsham,[1] her condescending behavior is not any better at such a crucial moment when that last hope is gone. Instead of understanding the students' search for questions and sympathizing with their shock, she is disdainful and self-complacent: "It's touching, Kathy, to see you so taken aback. It demonstrates, in a way, that we did our job well. As you say, why would anyone doubt you had a soul?" (255). She actually keeps insisting on taking care of the students as a job rather than as a humanitarian and ethical concern:

> I can see what I'm saying won't be welcome to you. But you mustn't be dejected. I hope you can appreciate how much we *were* able to secure for you. Look at you both now! You've had good lives, you're educated and cultured.
>
> (256; emphasis original)

In general, the tone is mocking and there is a contrast between the guardians' sense of entertainment at it all and the students' helplessness:

> It is edifying to see how the Hailsham activists had a good time in the movement, "cabinet ministers, bishops, all sorts of famous people coming to attend", while the clones were kept uninformed, or rather quite manipulatively misinformed on what was going on.
>
> (Hyvärinen 2008, 213)

As a consequence, this general lack of feelings toward the students turns also very ironic since society is demanding of them to possess a quality that humans themselves do not show. Besides, it is somehow pointless to try to secure inner virtues and capacities when their internal organs as such are not. As Lisa Fluet explains,

> Kathy H. and Tommy seem incapable of dwelling for too long upon the irony of their circumstances—here, as clones who hope that evidence of their capacity for real feelings before a human authority figure will defer surrender of their actual physical interiors to a largely unfeeling public
>
> (2007, 281)

This is the very same point Kathy had indirectly raised to the guardians at the beginning of their visit when intrigued about the finality of collecting and taking students' art:

> Why did we do all of that work in the first place? Why train us, encourage us, make us produce all of that? If we're just going to give donations anyway, then die, why all those lessons? Why all those books and discussions?
>
> (Ishiguro 2006/2005, 254)

In turn, Madame seems to express her remorse but remains halfway to admit her due responsibility: "'Poor creatures. What did we do to you? With all our schemes and plans?' [...] 'Miss Emily [...] You speak to them,' Madame said, as though washing her hands of everything" (249–50).

A further irony yet is how the impossibility of deferring completion is about to literally destroy Kathy and Tommy's lives but not their love. After the fatal revelation of more lies that crush the hope to fight against their imminent destinies, Kathy and Tommy leave and drive as "helpless souls" into the solitary night, as a reflection of their having been expelled. Indeed, Kathy seems to choose the "weird roads" on purpose considering their outsider status:

> I kept us on the most obscure back roads I knew, where only our headlights disturbed the darkness. We'd occasionally encounter other headlights, and then I'd get the feeling they belonged to other carers, driving home alone, or maybe like me, with a donor beside them. I realized, of course, that other people used these roads; but that night, it seemed to me these dark byways of the country existed just for *the likes of us*, while the big glittering motorways with their huge signs and super cafés were for everyone else.
>
> (267; emphasis added)

In turn, Tommy breaks down as a consequence of the news; he asks Kathy to stop the car and falls to the muddy floor, his face "distorted with fury", screaming "swear-words", "raging, shouting, flinging his fists and kicking out" (269). Kathy's love for Tommy still persists as she does not let go of him even in the adversity symbolized by the elements that obliterate them:

> I reached for his flailing arms and held on tight. He tried to shake me off, but I kept holding on, until he stopped shouting and I felt the fight go out of him. Then I realized he too had his arms around me. And so we stood together like that, at the top of that field, for what seemed like ages, not saying anything, just holding each other, while the wind kept blowing and blowing at us, tugging our clothes, and for a moment, it seemed like we were holding onto each other because that was the only way to stop us being swept away into the night.
>
> (269)

While Kathy perseveres in their union, Tommy also has a firm if different perception of love. Due to his advancing deteriorated state before his fourth donation, he prefers staying away from Kathy to spare her" suffering and his own as she witnesses his coming apart:

> "Ruth wanted that other thing for us," Tommy said. "She wouldn't necessarily have wanted you to be my carer through this last bit." [...] "Ruth

> wanted the other thing for us," Tommy repeated. "All this is something else. Kath, I don't want to be that way in front of you".
>
> (275)

When Kathy refuses and insists on continuing to care of him, Tommy replies by resorting again to the use of art and the imagination, creating a meaningful story that can serve as a farewell to Kathy and for his own coming to terms with his destiny:

> I keep thinking about this river somewhere, with the water moving really fast. And these two people in the water, trying to hold onto each other, holding on as hard as they can, but in the end it's just too much. The current's too strong. They've got to let go, drift apart. That's how I think it is with us. It's a shame, Kath, because we've loved each other all our lives. But in the end, we can't stay together forever.
>
> (277)

In short, after all hopes are apparently shattered, love and art remain profoundly connected. If the proof of someone's love was supposed to be revealed in their artwork, Tommy's story confirms that belief. In addition, he not only keeps drawing his mechanical animals but shows command of other forms of artistic expression to explain who he is and the fundamental mystery of "what lay ahead", that is, the death that drifts us all apart (262).

"Your Art Will Display Your *Souls*!"

As just discussed, love is connected to art, which in the novel is conceived as an expression of the clones' humanity and hence as another proof that could change their assigned role in society. The students' hope is that they can escape their last donation(s) and live for a few years longer, which putatively happens when a couple is in love and prove it. According to Tommy, there was a "way to judge" love: "that's why they took away our art [...] what she's [Madame] got reveals our souls. [...] That's why the Gallery was so important, and why the guardians wanted us to work so hard on our art and our poetry" (173–4). Although he is partially mistaken, his theory is far from non-sensical as it resonates with common views about the nature and possibilities of subjugated groups:

> the issue of souls is critical to old discourses of race and discrimination, in which we keep asking whether slaves, Africans, heathens, or women could have a soul. It is no coincidence that so many national projects have fought to document the artistic creativity of particular peoples.
>
> (Hyvärinen 2008, 213)

Due to this association of the concept of the soul to humanity and civilization, the concerned groups are especially interested in proving they have one. Added to this, in general, some interventionist plans are developed in certain societies, which are part of experiments and disciplinary practices by the state or well-intended associations or scientists, including the dominant elite of Hailsham in the case of *NLMG*. Tommy's trust is shattered only when Madame demystifies the idea that "your art will display your *souls*!'" (Ishiguro 2006/2005, 248; emphasis original) and concludes that such a "dream" of granting deferrals is outside their prospects (256). For the guardians, as seen earlier, the students' artwork is intended to improve students' miserable conditions but not to destabilize the underlying system that is responsible for their subjugation as clones, their suffering through donations and eventual premature death.

This is why children are encouraged to write poems, paint and produce other artifacts, with a view to create the best pieces to be selected and praised[2]: "If for us the Gallery remained in a hazy realm, what was solid enough fact was Madame's turning up usually twice – sometimes three or four times – each year to select from our best work" (32). As it turns out, art is a key element of coercion and control. That is to say, it is not only the guardians who judge artwork (and therefore the students) at given circumstances every year. Rather, this topic becomes also an everyday pressure. The importance of art is promulgated or exacerbated by students themselves, who take the matter very seriously and even seem to interiorize art's role as a means of exclusion: "A lot of time, how you were regarded at Hailsham, how much you were liked and respected, had to do with how good you were at 'creating'" (16). For instance, Tommy is brutally isolated and bullied by his peers on the grounds that he lacks due talent. After he had done a "deliberately childish" painting of an elephant (20), even though intended "as a kind of joke" (19), Tommy becomes stigmatized and rejected: "He got left out of games, boys refused to sit next to him at dinner, or pretended not to hear if he said anything in his dorm after lights-out" (20). As a consequence of this restrictive view of art, in which students are led to meet certain standards, Tommy's personal and social development is severely altered, developing "big temper tantrums" (20) and stopping to create anything for the rest of his childhood.

However, just the same as love, art provides students with some room for change and freedom away from society's conditioning. Only Miss Lucy seems to dissociate art from the functional standards held at Hailsham, when she talks to Tommy, whose drawings had been generally seen by both students and guardians as "rubbish" (105), about the value of his efforts to improve and the significance of being creative to develop one's identity: "Listen, Tommy, your art, it is important. And not just because it's evidence [for the Gallery]. But for your own sake. You'll get a lot from it, just for yourself" (106).

Moreover, the children's true creativity is not shown in the objects they are required to produce, but in the beliefs and fantasies they create to explain themselves or the world and the deeply personal reveries showing their individuality. This is shown, for example, in the recurrent use of theories to rationalize and understand their enigmatic environment or origins, and the creation of stories to express their intimate wishes, which is epitomized by Tommy's complex schemes or theories or by his final composition, as shown earlier, as well as by Kathy's important song. She becomes profoundly attached to music after she buys a cassette tape (called *Songs After Dark*, by Judy Bridgewater) at one of Hailsham's Sales when she's 11 and admits changing her favorite song's lyrics (the third track: "Never Let Me Go"), which she prefers to interpret according to her own yearnings:

> What was so special about this song? Well, the thing was, I didn't used to listen properly to the words; I just waited for that bit that went: "Baby, baby, never let me go…" And what I'd imagine was a woman who'd been told she couldn't have babies, who'd really, really wanted them all her life. Then there's a sort of miracle and she has a baby, and she holds this baby very close to her and walks around singing: "Baby, never let me go…" […] Even at the time, I realized this couldn't be right, that this interpretation didn't fit with the rest of the lyrics. But that wasn't an issue with me. The song was about what I said, and I used to listen to it again and again, on my own, whenever I got the chance.
>
> (70)

This appears as a sign of the character's creativity and latent free will since "by severing the lyric from its context and making the baby literal, Kathy is able to elaborate a deliberately erroneous, knowingly personal interpretation of an otherwise bland refrain" (Currie 2009, 92).

Following Bruce Robbins, the issue of myth-making is decidedly marked and functions as an indication of student's determination to transcend the way in which they are supposed to act and who they are thought to be:

> The irony, exquisitely compressed into this theology of provisional salvation, is that the school fails to recognize the children's genuine creativity, which expresses itself not in the artwork but rather in this myth-making about the artwork and its ability to transform their lives.
>
> (2007, 294)

Emily Johansen has also pointed out the transformative possibilities of the created narrative around the love relationship, which replaces or "exceeds the administrative narrative of carer–donor interaction" (2016, 9). She explains that eventually Tommy and Ruth somehow choose to project a new identity which differs from their assigned roles: "they narrate their existence through grand romance and exceptionality, rather than the language of meritorious reward that accompanies Kathy's opening summation of her job performance and its reflection of her subjectivity" (9). Besides, other creative inclinations, such as essay-writing on the part of Kathy "once [she is] not a carer anymore and [she has got] time" (Ishiguro 2006/2005, 114), reveal "that their urge to produce something of artistic and expressive value is not limited to the time when they are forced to do so" (Mašínová 2016, 59–60).

All in all, the characters live and act as if they can decide over their own destinies, even though they are simultaneously aware of their fate. They show a willingness to pursue their dreams which seems compatible with their being predestined, which is probably a natural way to live. This particularly explains Kathy's attitude in the last scene of the novel (see the epigraph), a few weeks after losing Tommy, which has been misinterpreted simply as a rejection to face her own death and conditions rather than as a regular attempt to go on despite all such circumstances:

> Kathy's tears are not for herself or her impending death. Instead, she weeps for the friends that she has "lost" [...] Kathy refuses to consider that her role as a living, breathing organ farm is a cause for emotional distress and even goes so far as to find comfort in the demands of her job. She braces herself after her emotional outburst, insisting that she was never "out of control", and then calmly drives off to wherever, according to her occupation, she is "supposed to be".
>
> (Eatough 2011, 132)

As Angel Tuohy reminds us In *Making Meaning: Death, Dignity, and Dasein in Kazuo Ishiguro's Never Let Me Go*, this "twin awareness and ignorance of the facts of nature, specifically death" is reflected "in our own real-world human lives" and adds that "this duality is what makes human existence bearable" (2020, 6). This shows the optimistic look for purpose in one's life, which explains the noteworthy role of hope in *NLMG*, including the belief in redemption which is manifested in love and art as well as religion. For example, the role of faith as a temporary escape and solace against the loss just experienced can be appreciated when Kathy resorts to the imagination or "fantasy", as she calls it. That final scene offers the last image of promise, particularly the belief in an afterlife or resurrection through the idea of return after death. She sees a fence of barbed wire in a field around which "all sorts of rubbish had caught and tangled" (Ishiguro 2006/2005, 282), an image which prompts her recollection of everything she has lost and could be salvaged, as she imagines it:

> the electrified wire that literally sends currents through the "stuff" caught up in its metal barbs is an affective register of the lifeline that rescues or re-cues "rubbish", [...] a kind of fishing reel of rescue that cuts across

> the verdant landscape vista of hope's horizon, pulling the promise of the distance point where wishes meet the ground of reality into the tangible midline [...] The lure of the fence is a call-and-response fantasy of love, one that promises return in every sense.
>
> (Casid 2012, 129).

A Road to Salvation: Religion, Determinism and Free Will

Apart from the resurrecting hope in the last part of the story, Kathy's decision to stop the fantasy has been also interpreted as her "tranquil" acceptance of death and the "impermanence of life" and so reflects the Buddhist concept of *Mujo*, which has been influential in Japanese literature and refers to the everchanging nature of the world (Taketomi 2018, 123). Religion is also present in how some characters believe in that "theology of provisional salvation", in Robbins' words (2007), associated with the possibility of escaping their immediate destinies of death and living longer if donations are postponed.

Furthermore, they generally try to look for an ultimate meaning in their lives, which is vividly described in how they confront their "creators"/the guardians in search of answers about both their past and destiny. On their visit to Madame and Miss Emily at the end, Kathy and Tommy can discover who they are, as another of the guardians, Miss Lucy, once suggested:

> Look, there are all kinds of things you don't understand, Tommy, and I can't tell you about them. Things about Hailsham, about your place in the wider world, all kinds of things. But perhaps one day, you'll try and find out. They won't make it easy for you, but if you want to, really want to, you might find out.
>
> (Ishiguro 2006/2005, 106)

Paradigmatically, the road to self-knowledge emphasizes the students' will and determination, as Lucy indicates, proving the existence of some room for autonomy instead of their total subjugation. Given that knowledge about the practice of cloning is quite veiled or inaccessible, the quest implies a challenge but ironically also becomes a means for validating their subjectivity and ability to resist that system. Even Ruth had initiated her own challenging search, in her case for Madame's address so that Kathy and Tommy might attempt to defer their organ donations, revealing that such an information was also beyond the boundaries established for the clones to know: "it wasn't easy. It took me a long time, and I ran a few risks. But I got it in the end, and I got it for you two. Now it's up to you to find her and try" (229).

Another important quest in the novel lies in "the clones' efforts to find their model 'normals'", or possibles, as they are called, which can be interpreted as if they were seeking their parents (Shaddox 2013, 455) or facing their "creators" once more, given the unequal relationship of power mainly portrayed. According to Tiffany Tsao's study of the "deeply theological nature" of the novel, biotechnological creation emulates a religious narrative around God's power over its creatures and "belies the apparent secularity of the social order featured" in it (2012, 215):

> Significant scientific advances in the world of *Never Let Me Go* have similarly elevated humans to the status of gods, endowing them not only with the ability to create life in their own image, but also with immortality, achieved by cutting their creations' lives short.
>
> (220)

Still, the students themselves do not feel completely helpless and there is in the novel a combination of determinism and free will, as in Christian doctrine that can admit the event of creation without diminishing individual action. Most of the students describe such a search for possibilities as a way to learn about their origins and future since, being clones, they think they are predestined not just to donate but to fulfill a certain profile. At the same time, as said earlier, they voluntarily want to confront that ultimate truth, which is more conveniently expressed by some of them in particular who conceive God/creation/cloning just as a punctual act (or "technical necessity"), which later lets them with the ability to choose for themselves in their lives:

> Then there were those questions about why we wanted to track down our models at all. One big idea behind finding your model was that when you did, you'd glimpse your future. [...] we all of us, to varying degrees, believed that when you saw the person you were copied from, you'd get some insight into who you were deep down, and maybe too, you'd see something of what your life held in store. There were some who thought it stupid to be concerned about possibles at all. Our models were an irrelevance, a technical necessity for bringing us into the world, nothing more than that. It was up to each of us to make of our lives what we could.
>
> (Ishiguro 2006/2005, 137–8)

This fundamental search and the above-mentioned struggles disprove that commonly held view about students' passivity discussed in chapter one. As some critics categorically put it, "they blindly accept their functional state of existence as determined by society. They do not consider the possibility of pursuing authentic lives [...] Not one of them ever questions their own existence" (de Villiers and Slabbert 2011, 92). As already shown, students not only have questions about their origins and destinies but do seek answers to those questions, which challenges the statement that "they resemble human characters in all aspects except their lack of prospective agency" (Rosenfeld 2021, 134).

It has been argued that the clones/students "embrace the roles carved out for them", citing how Kathy takes pride in being a "carer", whereas "Tommy describes himself as "a pretty good donor". Furthermore, even "the most pugnacious Ruth" finally seems to surrender or shows "resignation" in her "'I was pretty much ready when I became a donor. It felt right. After all, that's what we're *supposed* to be doing, isn't it?'" (de Villiers and Slabbert 2011, 92; emphasis original). Likewise, Kathy is believed to uncritically go to where she "was supposed to be", which is no other than her own preparation to become a donor, describing that new role as "just about right" (Tsao 2012, 224). However, as Tsao notes, "it would be all too easy to dismiss the clones' acceptance and even desire for purpose as misguided" (224). She explains that the sense of purpose is mostly a religious but also secular human belief to explain our origins and face mortality:

> the comfort the clones derive from fulfilling their purpose bears an all too unsettling resemblance to what we ourselves might say when we have discovered a sense of purpose for our own lives. [...] we share the same mentality: in our world, the negative connotations of words like "purposeless", "futile", "pointless", "aimless", and "useless" betray the value we ourselves place on living purposefully, pointedly, and usefully.
>
> (224)

Tsao concludes that "perhaps it is high time we considered the possibility that life can go on in a meaningful way, even when one has no reason to live" (230). More interestingly, she shifts the critical attention to how human behavior is depicted in the novel, contrary to most scholarship concentrating only on the "parallels between the clones and ourselves rather than the human characters and ourselves" (220). We *are supposed* to equally identify with the search for our place in the world and with our own practice of "playing God" through cloning:

> As a narrative about creatures in relation to their gods and about biotechnological creation, *Never Let Me Go* is uniquely positioned to offer insight into both religious life and biotechnology in our own world—our relationship with our own God/gods, as well as how we as gods relate to our creations—for the novel invites us to identify with both parties in the creature–creator relationship, the clones *and* the humans.
>
> (220; emphasis added)

Notes

1 It closed because of lack of funds.
2 Children get particularly excited and boast about their work being good enough to go "straight to the Galley" (32). Yet art also has a distinct value as it functions as a type of monetary means of circulation for the Sales, which was the means to get items outside of Hailsham:

> For each thing you put in, you were paid in Exchange Tokens—the guardians decided how many your particular masterpiece merited—and then on the day of the Exchange you went along with your tokens and 'bought' the stuff you liked. (16)

References

Baccolini, Raffaella. 2004. "The Persistence of Hope in Dystopian Science Fiction." *PMLA/Publications of the Modern Language Association of America* 119.3: 518–521.

Casid, Jill. 2012. "Handle with Care." *TDR/The Drama Review* 56.4: 121–135.

Ching Yi, Chung. 2016. "A Study of Loss and Memory in Kazuo Ishiguro." *Subaltern-speak: An International Journal of Postcolonial Studies* 4.3: 31–40.

Currie, Mark. 2009. "Controlling Time: *Never Let Me Go*." In *Kazuo Ishiguro: Contemporary Critical Perspectives*, edited by Sean Matthews and Sebastian Groes, 91–103. New York: Continuum.

de Villiers, Jan-Harm, and Magda Slabbert. 2011. "*Never Let Me Go*: Science Fiction and Legal Reality." *Literator: Journal of Literary Criticism, Comparative Linguistics and Literary Studies* 32.3: 85–103.

Eatough, Matthew. 2011. "The Time that Remains: Organ Donation, Temporal Duration, and Bildung in Kazuo Ishiguro's *Never Let Me Go*." *Literature and Medicine* 29.1: 132–160.

Fluet, Lisa. 2007. "Immaterial Labors: Ishiguro, Class, and Affect." *Novel: A Forum on Fiction* 40.3: 265–288.

Hyvärinen, Matti. 2008. "Friendship, Care, and Politics: Kazuo Ishiguro's *Never Let Me Go*." *Redescriptions: Political Thought, Conceptual History and Feminist Theory* 12.1: 202–223.

Ishiguro, Kazuo. 2006/2005. *Never Let Me Go*. Kent: Faber and Faber.

Johansen, Emily. 2016. "Bureaucracy and Narrative Possibilities in Kazuo Ishiguro's *Never Let Me Go*." *The Journal of Commonwealth Literature* 51.3: 416–431.

Mašínová, Petra. 2016. *Art, Love and what Makes us Humans in Kazuo Ishiguro's Literary Works*. MA Thesis. Masaryk University.

Robbins, Bruce. 2007. "Cruelty is Bad: Banality and Proximity in *Never Let Me Go*." *Novel* 40.3: 289–302.

Shaddox, Karl. 2013. "Generic Considerations in Ishiguro's *Never Let Me Go*." *Human Rights Quarterly* 35.2: 448–469.

Taketomi, Ria. 2018. "Reading *Never Let Me Go* from the Mujo Perspective of Buddhism." *American, British & Canadian Studies* 31.1: 114–128.

Toker, Leona, and Daniel Chertoff. 2008. "Reader Response and the Recycling of Topoi in Kazuo Ishiguro's *Never Let Me Go*." *Partial Answers: Journal of Literature and the History of Ideas* 6.1: 163–180.

Tsao, Tiffany. 2012. "The Tyranny of Purpose: Religion and Biotechnology in Ishiguro's *Never Let Me Go*." *Literature and Theology* 26.2: 214–232.

Tuohy, Angel. 2020. *Making Meaning: Death, Dignity, and Dasein in Kazuo Ishiguro's Never Let Me Go*. MA Thesis. Montclair State University.

4 "Speculative Memoir"

Blending Autobiography and Science Fiction

Memory, Identity and Writing: Generic Approaches to Interpret *Never Let Me Go*

Whereas Chapter 1 discussed the characters' identity formation as clones in light of prevailing economic, educational and cultural systems that benefitted from their subordinated status, this chapter concentrates on the specific function of memory, which is a key narrative device, as a tool to (de)construct their identity, showing once again that hopeful room for some agency argued in chapter three.

NLMG is fundamentally based on a constant dialogue with the past. "My name is Kathy H. I'm twenty-eight years old and I've spent most of my time not looking forward but looking back and what happened to us at Hailsham". These words, which correspond to the opening of the novel's adaptation to film (2010), perfectly reflect its general tone. In the novel, Kathy is 31 and simply affirms that she has been "a carer now for over eleven years" (Ishiguro 2006/2005, 3), that is, there is no such a catchy mention of her obstinate remembering of the past but this is exactly what she does throughout. The film has therefore captured the main message of the novel through that captivating voice-over, which gives us the desire to discover the life of this woman and the early mystery around the unknown issue of caring repeatedly mentioned.

In fact, only a few lines after she presents herself in the novel, Kathy unfolds the persistence of memories against which she has been often struggling: "There have been times over the years when I've tried to leave Hailsham behind, when I've told myself I shouldn't look back so much. But then there came a point when I just stopped resisting" (4–5). The reason that motivates her final surrender to the workings of memory is not accidental but directly related to her past. It happens at the moment when she thinks she has met a donor from Hailsham, the place she grew up in and which therefore triggers her nostalgic recollection[1]: "What he wanted was not just to hear

DOI: 10.4324/9781003530695-5

about Hailsham, but to *remember* Hailsham, just like it had been his own childhood" (5; emphasis original). From then onwards, the narrative oscillates between the present and the past, between the adult Kathy recollecting her life as a carer and the disparate flashbacks to different moments of her life, mainly her childhood at Hailsham and the "intermedium" passage at the Cottages.

Autobiography and memoir—first-person accounts in which someone recollects, orders and generally "makes sense" of their whole or part of their lives—tend to account for a certain verisimilitude of the events and experiences narrated. Hence, these genres are believed to rely on a certain degree of authenticity. Yet, the use of science fiction, particularly dystopia, immediately situates us in a decidedly fictive world which, although sometimes may appear very similar to our societies in a certain sense, has been clearly exaggerated for artistic or moral purposes. Furthermore, some memories can be often repressed or altered such as due to trauma or selectivity (Drąg 2014). For this reason,

> the main character, Kathy, has a retrospective monologue which is stilted due to the decay of her memory. This means that the credibility of her understanding and the redemption she seeks from the past is compromised as a result of her nonlinear summary. As such, the knowledge Kathy gains from her past is problematic. It is Kathy's desire for order that fuels her narrative, a literary strategy common in Ishiguro's writing.
>
> (Byer 2019, 71)

Ishiguro has precisely addressed this issue in many of his novels and commented on "the fallibility of memory" and the characters' tendency toward "conscious and unconscious evasion" (in Shaffer and Wong 2008, 38). He states that memory is a "terribly treacherous terrain" and that "the very ambiguities of memory" can lead to and explain the characters' self-deception (39).

Although memory can certainly have a testimonial function (Teo 2014), for many critics, the act of remembering one's own life represents a practice that goes "beyond [rescuing] the archive" of the past and is instead fundamentally a cultural process of ongoing construction of the self (Brockmeier 2015). Wojciech Drąg analyzes how many of Ishiguro's works attest to the common workings of memory, its "tangled, unreliable and essentially reconstructive nature—its dependance on the temporary needs of the ego" (2014, 177). Mark Currie also studies the unreliability of the first-person narrative voice, examining the narrative style mostly based on a "constant mediation of events by some act of recall later" (2009, 94). In this respect, there are many examples of the "evocation of future time in the narration that arouses the expectations of an as yet unexplained occurrence" (94) or of the "recollection of a recollection that is not agreed upon" (95). Finally, Andrew Bennet considers the limited knowledge of most of Ishiguro's characters about their lives and past as their vision is "partial, shrouded, self-deceiving, faulty" (2023, 6). He concludes that "a key thematic consideration" in the author's work is the creation of a "fallible, ignorant, self-deceiving, amnesiac, narrator protagonist" (6).

As a consequence, the use of autobiographical forms can never be understood according to notions of "truth" about what happens but rather as a malleable instrument of negotiation. This is especially obvious in *NLMG*, as when certainly Kathy affirms relying on a posteriori (re)constructions:

> But that's probably going too far; chances are, at the time, I noticed all these things without knowing what on earth to make of them. And if these incidents now seem full of significance and all of a piece, it's probably because I'm looking at them in the light of what came later.
>
> (Ishiguro 2006/2005, 77)

Other times, she simply prefers to hold a certain version of events for her own purposes: "Even at the time, I realized this couldn't be right, that this interpretation didn't fit with the rest of the lyrics. But that wasn't an issue with me. The song was about what I said" (70). In fact, Kathy's remembrance is fundamentally altered by her search for meaning and "subsequently acquired awareness" about past events: "She carefully scrutinizes her memories of Hailsham for harbingers of the students' fate [...] When reexamining those recollections, Kathy endows them with entirely new meanings, recognizing that [...] 'significance is hindsight'" (Drąg 2014, 177).

For the most part, Kathy makes use of an informal language which gives the impression of a spontaneously spoken narrative and situates it away from any complex literary artifice. However, she often presents herself as an unreliable narrator. Kathy repeatedly shows signs of not properly recalling her childhood and uses expressions that cast serious doubts about the verisimilitude of her narration. In general, she attributes self-doubt or flawed memories to the passing of time—"This was all a long time ago so I might have some of it wrong" (Ishiguro 2006/2005, 13)—, although sometimes she is unsure about her own feelings which she could be well misinterpreting—"For Ruth, for the others, it was that detached, and the chances are that's how it was for me too. Or maybe I'm remembering it wrong" (8). In addition, due to the fact that she is giving us only her own perspective, she is aware (and honest enough to admit) that others might remember things differently: "I'm not sure [...] My own memory of it is that" (21). This recurrent feature exposes the limits of Kathy's narrative as a truthful account, which is due to her flawed and repressed memory but also intensified by the very context of coercion and secrecy she has lived in:

> The reader, being dependent on Kathy's narration, which draws on her imperfect and, therefore, inevitably flawed reflections, has to read between the lines to make sense of the situation. The same applies to Kathy and the other students who are left to interpret their lives, relying only on their limited, censored and superimposed frames of reference.[2]
>
> (De Villiers and Slabbert 2011, 89)

What is certain, however, is that the use of an introspective first-person narration helps the reader to identify and empathize with the character's own thoughts and feelings.[3] The use of the memoir genre is acknowledged to generate empathy:

> The organizing of the novel as a memoir humanizes the situation of characters who are not even thought of as being human. The insights it provides of Kathy's and her friends' inner emotions, love stories and childlike desires allow the reader to empathize with them.
>
> (Bizzini 2013, 75)

This is combined with meta-references and direct allusions to the audience, which is constructed as Kathy's contemporaries to reinforce the connection: "the readers' sympathy with the narrator is further reinforced by the narrator's direct address to the reader who is also, implicitly, a 'carer'" (Toker and Chertoff 2008, 168).

It is therefore difficult to establish generic boundaries as to the nature of Ishiguro's text, as many critics have already pinpointed. For example, some of the most noted variations or "violations" of genre conventions is that dystopic fiction is not set in the future but in the immediate past (as indicated by the single note in a page prefacing the text: "England, late 1990s") and that there is no use of technological or scientific language (Shaddox 2013), unlike the classic futurist and high-tech scenarios of other famous dystopian science fiction novels with which it has been usually compared (such as *Brave New World* (1932) by Aldous Huxley or *1984* (1949) by George Orwell). Furthermore, whereas dystopias tend to take place in invented or displaced geographical settings, *NLMG* is set in an alternate England, which, as has been remarked, is uncannily familiar (Garland-Thomson 2019; Toker and Chertoff, 2008).

Gabriele Griffin has analyzed how criticism "puzzled over the novel's genre", quoting some of the reviews that identified it, for example, "as an unusual piece of nightmarish science fiction blended with an evocative reworking of the traditional boarding-school story" (2009, 645). Griffin also expresses her own surprise at another critical reception: "this novel will be described as science fiction.

But there's no science here" (645). Griffin sustains that science runs as a subtext in *NLMG* due to the context in which it was written, and is more interested in how the presence of science figures as a "cultural imaginary" than in how it appears particularly in the novel: "*Never Let Me Go* (2005) was gestated [...] and appeared first during a period—the early 2000s—when cloning, and biotechnological developments and debates associated with these more generally, were high on the public agenda" (646).[4]

In this sense, another useful distinction is to replace the frequently used label science fiction for that of "speculative fiction", which defines writing based on "real scientific and technological breakthroughs" (Arias 2011, 380). *NLMG* is thus compared to other dystopias such as Margaret Atwood's which explore existing scientific dilemmas or try to envision the limits to "the furthering of knowledge" due to "the growing public concern over the unforeseen results of current advances in the life sciences" (380). In fact, there are ongoing studies as to how scientific and/or realistic are the speculative fictions of writers like Ishiguro (Petrillo 2014; Volpone 2020) and Atwood (Devanny 2022), among others. Furthermore, the term slipstream, coined in 1989, has become popular to describe contemporary texts that defy the boundaries between reality and science fiction as well as confusingly mix genre conventions (Davis 2012; Frelik 2011).

In general, "landmark" science fiction works from the twentieth century onwards "offer a critique of how we live and who we are now" (Rosenfeld 2005, 40). Nonetheless, according to Karl Shaddox, *NLMG* "eschews dystopian literature's usual sociopolitical didactics and polemics" (2013, 449)[5]; and the author Ishiguro himself seems uninterested in setting alarmist messages or warnings against the ethical or scientific implications of advanced experiments such as cloning in this case, as much as his text has been associated with the first cloning of a living being (sheep Dolly) only some years before its publication in 2005 (Mirsky 2006, 629).[6] Rather, the text was intended as a reflection on human mortality, as several critics have equally noted. For example, according to Barry Lewis, "*Never Let Me Go* is not hard-core sci-fi, but rather a tale that borrows certain themes and trappings of the genre to explore perennial issues about the human condition" (2011, 200). Virginia Yeung has also stated that "mirroring human experience in an intensified way, the characters live in the shadow of death" (2017, 1), and Ishiguro himself announced:

> I suppose, ultimately, I wanted to write a book about how people accept that we are mortal and we can't get away from this, and that after a certain point we are all going to die, we won't live forever [...] I wanted the characters in *Never Let Me Go* to react to this horrible programme they seem to be subjected to in much the way in which we accept the human condition, accept ageing, and falling to bits, and dying.
>
> (in Matthews 2009, 124)

In fact, Ishiguro's novel is profoundly philosophical and he tries to make the audience delve into existentialist questions about mortality, identity, free will and life uncertainty, as the author has also disclosed in a different interview:

> having clones as central characters made it very easy to allude to some of the oldest questions in literature; questions which in recent years have become a little awkward to raise in fiction. "What does it mean to be human?" "What is the soul?" "What is the purpose for which we've been created?"
>
> (in Mullan 2006, n.p.)

In this respect, the film again has perfectly captured this existentialist message and made it more explicit by modifying the ending. The book portrays Kathy fantasizing about seeing Tommy again "only a couple of weeks since [she]'d lost him" (Ishiguro 2006/2005, 282), but also realistically accepting their destinies, particularly her waiting for her own upcoming donation: "though the tears rolled down my face, I wasn't sobbing or out of control. I just waited a bit, then turned back to the car, to drive off to wherever it was I was supposed to be" (282). The film does not contemplate exclusively the clones' plight and deliberately meditates on the parallelism with humans when facing death: "What I'm not sure about, is if our lives have been so different from the lives of the people we save. We all complete. Maybe none of us really understand what we've lived through, or feel we've had enough time" (Romanek 2010).

As a matter of fact, in an encounter with the film actors, Ishiguro confirmed this interpretation using very similar words, again declaring his interest with addressing mortality, the "human condition" or "human existence": "I was looking for a metaphor we face mortality and we can't really escape from that. We can't escape from the fact that we've only got a limited amount of time" (Film Independent 2010). He even declares that the theme of cloning was secondary, which downplays the question of how the novel has been mostly received or how it fits into a particular genre:

> I was always looking for that [the fact that our existence is limited]. What you might call the sci-fi speculative surface was almost like the last thing; it was the last piece of the jigsaw. It was almost like a device to make the thing work. That was the idea, but inevitably then, having chosen this dystopian world it starts to raise all these issues about biotechnology, perhaps about organ donation. That's fine with me.
>
> (Film Independent 2010)

Aside from authorial intentionality, it is perfectly possible to critically read *NLMG* from a social and moral perspective which does not preclude the importance of its underlying philosophy.[7] As a case in point, Rosemarie

Garland-Thomson has examined the ethical implications not only about cloning but also organ trafficking while also retaining the deeper literary value and message: "The novel's rich blend of dystopian science fiction, literary naturalism, magical realism, and elegy pose significant moral and philosophical questions. At the heart of Ishiguro's novel is a subtle and complicated exploration of our psycho-emotional response to mortality" (2019, 30).

In short, *NLMG* escapes easy classification, showing instead a distinctive blurring of categories. In this sense, Keith McDonald has particularly studied the text's borrowing of multiple literary conventions. For example, he has identified the feature of blending autobiography and dystopia through the term "speculative memoir" (2007). The choice of memoir, a popular form that emerged in the 1990s, seems adequate for a dystopian narrative as it has been commonly employed to narrate experiences of trauma such as the events depicted in the novel *NLMG*.[8] McDonald additionally proposes going "beyond its autobiographical frame" and concentrates on its reliance on the genre of pathography, that is, "the writing of corporeal decline and the affects [*sic*] of illness on others" (80), given that Kathy's narrative mostly deals with the tragic destinies she and her friends face(d).

Other critics have acknowledged the use of different first-person narratives as a means of coping with a traumatic experience. For example, storytelling figures "not only [as] a transmission of personal memories, but also a way of giving voice back to those who died. Recollecting the legacy of previous generations [...] is a way of fighting back barbarism" (Bizzini 2013, 70). This analysis about the resort to storytelling in the "trauma narrative" relies on the therapeutic potential of language to heal (Levy 2011). Following Yeung, memory is also used to "assuage the psychic trauma of mortality" (2017, 1). As Kathy herself puts it, memory can defy death: "the memories I value most, I don't see them ever fading. I lost Ruth, then I lost Tommy, but I won't lose my memories of them" (Ishiguro 2006/2005, 280).

At the very beginning of her account, Kathy admits "getting this urge to order all these old memories" (37). Remembering is not only paramount but also serves to provide a circular structure to *NLMG*. One of the reasons lies in the fact that Kathy is facing "premature ageing" (Charlwood 2018, 88), which means she is particularly compelled to retrieve her life when confronted with her upcoming death. Aaron Rosenfeld has labeled *NLMG* as an "anti-bildungsroman" for the way in which it "inverts [the classic novel of formation] in order to articulate a journey of un-becoming" (2021, 112). This explains why the text is mostly structured through flashbacks that trace the (de)formation of identity typical in the genre: "Understanding dystopian character requires an understanding not just of who characters are, but of who they fail to become, and how" (112). It is therefore necessary to explore the literary strategies used to convey that vital path of (un)becoming, particularly the representation of trauma and nostalgia.

The (De)Formation of Identity in *Never Let Me Go:* Representing Trauma and Nostalgia

Apart from flashbacks, one of the main features of *NLMG* is its delayed narration, that is, the use of a nonlinear and rumbling temporal framework that suspends the main mystery or message: the revelation that the students are clones and their own awareness of such a significant fact, which happens at about page 80 in the novel. This device of clearly differentiating the story and the plot is not only intended to intensify readers' attention and interest but is particularly appropriate to mirror Kathy's arduous process of remembrance, especially in relation to the "web of secrets and half-truths" of her school years (Hyvärinen 2008, 207). Her memory is particularly fragmented since her life resembles a puzzle in which she is progressively finding answers or the missing pieces about what they have not been told (yet), as one of the guardians (Miss Lucy)[9] tells the students when trying to disclose who they really are: "you've been told and not told" (Ishiguro 2006/2005, 79).

The time and effort taken for self-discovery reflects the general buildup of adolescent/adult identity but is also believed to be a studied strategy so that students better conform: "The main educational technique through which the students are brought to accept their fate consists of causing awareness of it to grow upon them gradually—as it similarly gradually grows upon the reader" (Toker and Chertoff 2008, 168). This interpretation is backed by Tommy's "theory" about "'the told and not told' idea" (Ishiguro 2006/2005, 81), that is, the way in which the necessary repression or manipulation of knowledge for the students to acquiesce is carefully handled:

> Tommy thought it possible that the guardians had, throughout all our years at Hailsham, timed very carefully and deliberately everything they told us, so that we were always just too young to understand properly the latest piece of information. But of course we'd take it in at some level, so that before long all this stuff was there in our heads without us ever having examined it properly.
>
> (81)

Kathy defines it "like a conspiracy theory" but admits that "there's probably something in it", which could explain why she cannot recall when exactly she learned she was a clone:

> Certainly, it feels like I *always* knew about donations in some vague way, even as early as six or seven. And it's curious, when we were older and the guardians were giving us those talks, nothing came as

> a complete surprise. It *was* like we'd heard everything somewhere before.
>
> (81; original emphasis)

This brainwashing, a trope that appears in science fiction, from an early age guarantees that students naturally admit (and even joke about) donations and "accept their fates unquestioningly":

> All the students know they'll never reach middle age. Yet they study and gossip like they've nothing to worry about because they are used to that fact, having had it told to them before they could fully fathom it. By the time they're thirteen, they've developed a running joke of "unzipping" themselves (pretending to unzip their skin, remove an organ, and zip their skin back up again) as a way of acknowledging their futures.
>
> (Cappo 2009, 48)

The first significant moment of (de)formation in which the students learn about their predetermined lives occurs precisely when the transition to adulthood they expect is shut. As any child, they want to pursue different occupations and trajectories in life, but their dreams are shattered upon learning about their condition(ing):

> None of you will go to America, none of you will be film stars. And none of you will be working in supermarkets as I heard some of you planning the other day. Your lives are set out for you. You'll become adults, then before you're old, before you're even middle-aged, you'll start to donate your vital organs. That's what each of you was created to do. You're not like the actors you watch on your videos, you're not even like me. You were brought into this world for a purpose, and your futures, all of them, have been decided.
>
> (Ishiguro 2006/2005, 80)

After that, the novel delves into the characters' quest to find their "possibles" or the humans from which they were presumably "modeled from" (137). This is a fundamental search for one's origins which is attributed an important transcendental meaning by most of the students:

> we all of us, to varying degrees, believed that when you saw the person you were copied from, you'd get *some* insight into who you were deep down, and maybe too, you'd see something of what your life held in store.
>
> (137–8, original emphasis).

Such a quest for a meaningful and singular identity is never allowed. Other instances in which students' identity is (de)formed show us their clear dehumanization by means of animalization, such as when they are repeatedly seen as "spiders" (35, 243, 263), and objectification: the "progression of the students' lives" is marked by the word "complete", "invoking the image of an object fulfilling its purpose" (De Villiers and Slabbert 2011, 91). Furthermore, their development is dramatically halted by premature death which is not only inevitable but required to serve the purpose of donations:

> *Never Let Me Go* depicts its clone characters literally disassembled. By our standards they are human. They think, feel, and act, negotiating adolescence and early adulthood with grace and sensitivity. But by the standards of their society they are freerange spare parts. While Ishiguro develops character, he subtracts from his novel the possibility of mature adulthood toward which the novel of formation conduces.
>
> (Rosenfeld 2021, 115)

Not only the characters' development is dramatically cut off in a literal and figurative sense, but they are forced to face additional suffering in their role as carers, which is another form of trauma as indirect victims:

> being a witness of the violence and death is the root of her trauma. Kathy even witnessed the painful struggle of her friend Ruth before her death. [...] This is the only place in the novel that directly involves the tragic death of a cloned [in which a] few simple descriptions hint to us the violent characteristics of organ donation and the immense suffering of the dead. For Kathy, this means serious psychological trauma.
>
> (Yan-Ling 2021, 89)

In fact, the representation of trauma does not figure as straight coercion but as more subtle consequences in identity and memory. This is particularly altered by a profound sense of loss after Kathy experiences her friends' death. For example, "much of what Kathy remembers about Hailsham is created anew in the light of the dramatically changed circumstances of her bereavement" (Drąg 2014, 177). The idealized memories she holds about her childhood produce a kind of shelter, corresponding to a "nostalgic past" (or "Paradise lost") which functions as an "antithesis of the conflicted and profoundly disappointing present" (164, 177–8). This romantic reconstruction of early memories in the aftermath of loss also explains the prevailing elegiac tone:

> *Never Let Me Go* is no sci-fi thriller, however, but rather an elegy haunted with a melancholic longing for the lost innocence of the idyllic childhood

> lived at Hailsham, as well as the lost companions, friends, and lovers who have "completed" by the end of the story – as the narrator herself will soon do.
>
> (Garland-Thomson 2019, 32)

Of course, Kathy's preferred vision contrasts with the purposely fabricated past she must be equally aware of, as explicitly recounted by Miss Emily about the essence of Hailsham:

> You see, we were able to give you something, something which even now no one will ever take from you, and we were able to do that principally by *sheltering* you. [...] Yes, in many ways we *fooled* you. I suppose you could even call it that. But we sheltered you during those years, and we gave you your childhoods.
>
> (Ishiguro 2006/2005, 262–3; emphasis original)

This confession entails the tragic realization for the characters of the fact that not even their memories of their childhood belong to them, and Miss Emily admits that students were "protected" so that their "happiness" wouldn't be "shattered" (263). However, as said above, nostalgia becomes an anti-dote to trauma. Unlike general negative views of nostalgia as a signifier of paralysis (the idea that someone is "stuck in the past"),[10] in *NLMG* it appears as a possibility for the students to acquire a sense of belonging and personal integrity: "it is the memory of a happy past, associated with childhood years and home, that could restore their selves" (Dzhumaylo 2009, 83). Ishiguro has also clarified why the depiction of memory is particularly optimistic or "more benevolent" in *NLMG*, as compared to his previous novels, by saying that it is "principally a source of consolation" for the characters' tragic destiny (in Drąg 2014, 179).

According to Olga Dzhumaylo's analysis of the recurrence of wounds as metaphors of trauma, there is a strong connection between the disappearing of memory as such and the literal blurring of the characters' identity. For example, it seems no coincidence that when Ruth and Tommy are approaching their death, the former "continued pretending to remember nothing" (199), while the latter compares Hailsham to the ruins of a boat and shows himself quite indifferent: "It wouldn't be so bad, if it's like this [crumbling] now" (2009, 221). By contrast, Kathy's persistence to cling to her most cherished memories both relieves her pain and, more than anything, *determines* who she is.

Drawing on Drąg's notion of the "ethical potential of nostalgia" (183), Kathy's "attachment to Hailsham [...] continues to occupy a uniquely privileged position in her consciousness and remains the supreme attribute of her self-definition and an ever-accessible retreat from the present" (183). In other words, her tribute and reworking of memory provides a version of self not imposed by others but created by her own standards. This explains Kathy's "authentic engagement with the past" (183). In this respect, (re)constructing and retelling her life emerges as a key act of resistance against her supposed determinism, away from a "received and stereotyped account of the past" (183). Furthermore, Kathy's assessment of the past with the hindsight of her adult self also motivates her desire of action and change, such as her efforts to "'repair' the damage of past actions" (183), or to improve the relationship with friends (notably with Ruth). As a consequence, memory becomes fundamental in her journey of (un) becoming and the search in which identity is not to be found in the future but in the past.

Notes

1 It is the narrator's "ur-place", "her place of origin and the foundation of her identity", whose eventual disappearance represents the crumbling of Kathy's world, adding to the important loss of her own friends (Drąg 2014, 189).
2 Matti Hyvärinen has also remarked on the students' obvious limited knowledge due to censorship of information (such as the type of novels allowed to read), stating how "the children lived constantly within a tangled and complicated web of lies, paranoia and strictly controlled information" (2008, 219).
3 Note that this choice seems to be an aesthetic feature in most of Ishiguro's works, as well as the narrators-protagonists' retrieval of the past in a nostalgic and elegiac way (Shaffer 1998, 7).
4 Public anxieties about the "legal and ethical implications" surrounding the cloning of the adult sheep Dolly in 1995 motivated the 1997 report "Cloning Human Beings", by the National Bioethics Advisory Commission for the US (US Congress 1997, 1). In the subject about the "Potential Applications in Organ and Tissue Transplantation", it stated that "the notion of human cloning to produce individuals solely as organ donors is repugnant, almost unimaginable, and morally unacceptable" (30).
5 In *Dystopian Literature: A Theory and Research Guide*, Keith Cooker, who examines a considerable selection of utopian and dystopian literature (as well as films), affirms that the latter generally "constitutes a critique of existing social conditions or political systems" (1994, 3).
6 In the interview "Onscreen, Ishiguro's Sci Fi Novel is No Mere Clone", he also acknowledges not to follow particular literary conventions: "I worry less about categories and genres, you know. [...] all right, you want to call it science fiction, fine, but I mean, it might not fulfill a lot of the genre expectations of sci-fi fans" (NPR 2010, n.p.).
7 Cfr. for an existentialist and legal reading, which admits the distance between artistic and critical frameworks: "it is not Ishiguro's intention to consider a specific legal framework in *Never Let Me Go*, yet he indirectly raises and highlights the problematic nature of current medico-legal issues such as cloning [and] organ donations" (De Villiers and Slabbert 2011, 100).
8 As this chapter intends to show, *NLMG* offers a clear representation of trauma, even though this novel has been dismissed from such an analysis which only considers the author's historical fictions about World War II or Japan's invasion (Guo 2012).

9 As a matter of fact, Miss Lucy believes that Hailsham students should know about their fate, contrary to the school's policy and particularly Miss Emily, who prefers to keep children ignorant about the issue.
10 Nostalgia also tends to be associated with "escapism" and a "conservative" outlook against change (Drąg 2014, 183).

References

Arias, Rosario. 2011. "Life After Man? Posthumanity and Genetic Engineering in Margaret Atwood's *Oryx and Crake* and Kazuo Ishiguro's *Never Let Me Go*." In *Restoring the Mystery of the Rainbow: Literature's Refraction of Science*, edited by Valeria Tinkler-Villani and C.C. Barfoot, 379–394. Amsterdam: Brill.

Bennett, Andrew, ed. 2023. *The Cambridge Companion to Kazuo Ishiguro*. New York: Cambridge University Press.

Bizzini, Silvia Caporale. 2013. "Recollecting Memories, Reconstructing Identities: Narrators as Storytellers in Kazuo Ishiguro's *When We Were Orphans* and *Never Let Me Go*." *Atlantis* 35.2: 65–80.

Brockmeier, Jens. 2015. *Beyond the Archive: Memory, Narrative, and the Autobiographical Process*. Oxford: Oxford University Press.

Byer, Tia. 2019. "Speculative Fiction, Memory and Genetic Engineering in Kazuo Ishiguro's *Never Let Me Go*." *European Journal of Literature, Language and Linguistics Studies* 3.1: 70–76.

Cappo, Emily. 2009. *Repression and Displacement in Kazuo Ishiguro's When We Were Orphans and Never Let Me Go*. PhD Diss. University of Michigan.

Charlwood, Catherine. 2018. "'Stop… and Remember': Memory and Ageing in Kazuo Ishiguro's Novels." *American British & Canadian Studies* 31.1. 86–113.

Cooker, Keith. 1994. *Dystopian Literature: A Theory and Research Guide*. Westport: Greenwood Press.

Currie, Mark. 2009. "Controlling time: *Never Let Me Go*." In *Kazuo Ishiguro: Contemporary Critical Perspectives*, edited by Sean Matthews and Sebastian Groes, 91–103. New York: Continuum.

Davis, Doug. 2012. "Understanding Slipstream Fiction." *A Virtual Introduction to Science Fiction*: 1–8.

Devanny, Laura-Jane. 2022. "'Speculative Slipstreaming': The Impact of Literary Interventions within Contemporary Science Fiction." *Humanities* 11.5: 116–128.

De Villiers, Jan-Harm, and Magda Slabbert. 2011. "*Never Let Me Go*: Science Fiction and Legal Reality." *Literator: Journal of Literary Criticism, Comparative Linguistics and Literary Studies* 32.3: 85–103.

Drąg, Wojciech. 2014. "Seeking Refuge in Paradise Lost." In *Revisiting Loss: Memory, Trauma and Nostalgia in the Novels of Kazuo Ishiguro*, edited by Wojciech Drag, 164–184. Newcastle: Cambridge Scholars Publishing.

Dzhumaylo, Olga. 2009. "'Never-Let-Me-Go' Wounds: Leitmotifs in Kazuo Ishiguro's Novels." In *Textual Intricacies: Essays on Structure and Intertextuality in Nineteenth and Twentieth Century Fiction in English*, edited by Christiane Bimberg, 73–102. Trier: Wissenschaftlicher Verlag Trier.

Film Independent. 2010. "Kazuo Ishiguro Discusses his Intention Behind Writing the Novel *Never Let Me Go*." Available at: https://www.youtube.com/watch?v=_jCB59pPG7k&ab_channel=FilmIndependent

Frelik, Paweł. 2011. "Of Slipstream and Others: SF and Genre Boundary Discourses." *Science Fiction Studies* 38.1: 20–45.

Garland-Thomson, Rosemarie. 2019. "World Building, Citizenship, and Disability: The Strange World of Kazuo Ishiguro's *Never Let Me Go*." In *The Palgrave Handbook of Disability and Citizenship in the Global South*, 27–43. Cham: Palgrave Macmillan.

Griffin, Gabriele. 2009. "Science and the Cultural Imaginary: The Case of Kazuo Ishiguro's *Never Let Me Go*." *Textual Practice* 23.4: 645–663.

Guo, Deyan. 2012. "Trauma, Memory and History in Kazuo Ishiguro's Fiction." *Theory & Practice in Language Studies* 2.12: 2508–2516.

Huxley, Aldous. 1932. *Brave New World*. New York: Harper & Brothers.

Hyvärinen, Matti. 2008. "Friendship, Care, and Politics: Kazuo Ishiguro's *Never Let Me Go*." *Redescriptions: Political Thought, Conceptual History and Feminist Theory* 12.1: 202–223.

Ishiguro, Kazuo. 2006/2005. *Never Let Me Go*. Kent: Faber and Faber.

Levy, Titus. 2011: "Human Rights Storytelling and Trauma Narrative in Kazuo Ishiguro's *Never Let Me Go*." *Journal of Human Rights* 10: 1–16.

Lewis, Barris. 2011. "The Concertina Effect: Unfolding Kazuo Ishiguro's *Never Let Me Go*." In *Kazuo Ishiguro: New Critical Visions of the Novels*, edited by Sebastian Groes and Barry Lewis, 199–210. London: Red Globe Press.

Matthews, Sean. 2009: "'I'm Sorry I Can't Say More:' An Interview with Kazuo Ishiguro." In *Kazuo Ishiguro. Contemporary Critical Perspectives*, edited by Sean Matthews and Sebastian Groes, 114–125. New York: Continuum.

McDonald, Keith. 2007. "Days of Past Futures: Kazuo Ishiguro's *Never Let Me Go* as 'Speculative Memoir'." *Biography* 30.1: 74–83.

Mirsky, Marvin. 2006. "Notes on Reading Kazuo Ishiguro's *Never Let Me Go*." *Perspectives in Biology and Medicine* 49.4: 628–630.

Mullan, John. 2006. "Future Imperfect. Guardian Book Club with John Mullan." Available at: https://www.theguardian.com/books/2006/mar/25/featuresreviews.guardianreview36 ED 09/2010.

NPR. 2010. "Onscreen, Ishiguro's Sci-Fi Novel is No Mere Clone, All Things Considered." Available at http://www.npr.org/templates/story/story.php?storyId=129880145

Orwell, George. New York: Signet 1949. *1984*.

Petrillo, Stephanie. 2014. "Moral Theories and Cloning in Kazuo Ishiguro's *Never Let Me Go*." *Berkeley Undergraduate Journal* 27.1: 45–62.

Robbins, Bruce. 2007: "Cruelty is Bad: Banality and Proximity in Never Let Me Go." *Novel* 40.3: 289–302.

Romanek, Mark, dir. 2010. *Never Let Me Go*. Fox Searchlight Pictures.

Rosenfeld, Aaron. 2005. "Re-membering the Future: Doris Lessing' Experiment in Autobiography." *Critical Survey* 17.1: 40–55.

Rosenfeld, Aaron. 2021. "Dystopia and the End of Character in Zamyatin, Burgess, and Ishiguro." In *Character and Dystopia: The Last Men*, 112–148. New York: Routledge.

Shaddox, Karl. 2013. "Generic Considerations in Ishiguro's *Never Let Me Go*." *Human Rights Quarterly* 35.2: 448–469.

Shaffer, Brian. 1998. *Understanding Kazuo Ishiguro*. Columbia: University of South Carolina Press.

Shaffer, Brian, and Cynthia Wong, eds. 2008. *Conversations with Kazuo Ishiguro*. Jackson: University Press of Mississippi.

Teo, Yugin. 2014. "Testimony and the Affirmation of Memory in Kazuo Ishiguro's *Never Let Me Go*." *Critique: Studies in Contemporary Fiction* 55.2: 127–137.

Toker, Leona, and Daniel Chertoff. 2008. "Reader response and the recycling of topoi in Kazuo Ishiguro's *Never Let Me Go*." *Partial Answers: Journal of Literature and the History of Ideas* 6.1: 163–180.

US Congress. 1997. "Cloning Human Beings: Report and Recommendations of the National Bioethics Advisory Commission." National Bioethics Advisory Commission.
Volpone, Annalisa. 2020. "Supposing the Law: Nomos and Categorical Imperatives in *Never Let Me Go*." *Pólemos* 14.1: 73–90.
Yan-ling, G. O. N. G. 2021. "Traumatic Memories in Kazuo Ishiguro's *Never Let Me Go*." *Journal of Literature and Art Studies* 11.2: 88–91.
Yeung, Virginia. 2017. "Mortality and Memory in Kazuo Ishiguro's *Never Let Me Go*." *Transnational Literature* 9.2: 1–13.

Index

For Product Safety Concerns and Information please contact our EU
representative GPSR@taylorandfrancis.com
Taylor & Francis Verlag GmbH, Kaufingerstraße 24, 80331 München, Germany

www.ingramcontent.com/pod-product-compliance
Lightning Source LLC
LaVergne TN
LVHW010942110826
845149LV00013B/2721